Love Notes
Letters from Parents to Children
Anthony Segil

Love Notes
Letters from Parents to Children

First edition, 2016

www.SegilLoveNotes.com

A word of thanks –

To each parent, grandparent and child that contributed to this project, I wish to offer my deepest gratitude. Thank you for sharing a little piece of your heart and your mind, and your joy with the rest of the world through this book. May your words help to spread a little more comfort, a little more love, and a little more wisdom onto this planet we call home.

Anthony Segil

Contents

Foreword

Life is messy. There's no prescribed path, few guarantees, and no consensus on the purpose of it all. And that's what makes it beautiful, because therein lies all of the possibility.

Children understand this innately. Snowmen and sandcastles are impermanent except in the memory of their construction—it's the creation that makes the process joyful, not the project's endurance. For all of the birthday parties, family vacations, and other orchestrated memory-making occasions, it's the small moments that endure, like barreling down a sledding hill, crashing through the ocean waves, or just snuggling together at the end of a long day. For whatever challenges children encounter, willingly or otherwise, it is the warmth, safety, and comfort of a parent's love that sustains and restores them. In fact, it's all that children really need.

Parents understand that the manifestations of love take many forms—that it's not all swing sets, balloons, and chocolate ice cream. Love means battling to get that last bit of broccoli eaten. It means punishing bad behavior. It means anguish over quadratic equations. It means sitting beside a hospital bed in the middle of the night, frantic about what the morning might bring but hiding that fear under a third recitation of Green Eggs and Ham. Surviving hurt feelings and broken hearts is part of the territory, too.

As good as most of us are at showing children our love, telling them doesn't always come as easily. Especially as the ego and hormones of adolescence obscure and impair teenagers' minds and bodies, messages get confused and patience wanes. Advice sounds preachy, rules breed resentment, warnings rile fury, and wisdom is dismissed as antiquated nostalgia.

No matter how clear or straight a path we want to forge for our children, as parents we have to remember what our children already know. It's a certain amount of peril that makes life exciting. That failures fortify our resolve. That disappointments help us be grateful. That almost nothing lasts forever. Most of all, we have to remember that we're not alone.

Love Notes is meant to bridge the gaps between the love we show and the love we struggle to explain. This is a collection of more than fifty letters from parents from all walks of life, from the past and present, and on all of life's occasions. The common thread among them is love in all its crazy forms. Parents will be gratified to know that other parents feel like they do when it comes to their children. Children—and we're all somebody's child—may be surprised but will also take comfort in knowing this: Good parents are universally saying and doing the same things, which sometimes embarrass us but ultimately assure us of how wonderful and cherished we are.

Saying the words "I love you" is so vitally important, but the spoken words along don't convey the full depth and complexity of our emotions and intentions. Writing them down ensures that, not only do we say what we intend, but the words demand to be read. Letters ensure that thoughts truly get through, and hopefully passed down.

This is not to say that letter-writing is easy. I think the fear of sounding silly or dumb—the fear of not getting it "right" the first time—is what keeps parents (really, any of us) from putting pen to paper or fingers to keyboard. Sure, it takes some time spent staring at the blank page or screen. And yes, it means committing ideas and sentiments to the permanent record instead of letting words float off into the ephemera. But parents value legacy—it's one of the chief motivations for procreation, after all.

As you'll see in this book, letter-writing doesn't require eloquence. These letters have only been given the lightest editing, only to ensure that their messages aren't impeded by errant, unwieldy syntax. The human heart knows no rules of punctuation, after all. Please enjoy the letters as much as I have while compiling this anthology. Even more importantly, please accept the invitation at the close of this book to write your own letter to those you hold dear. You'll never, ever regret it.

To kick off, I will share with you the letter I wrote to my children, followed the letter that sowed the seed for this project, from Rabbi Lord Jonathan Sacks to his children. I hope you enjoy this labor of love.

With love,
Anthony Segil

A Letter to My Children

- Anthony Segil

Jameson, Flynn and Natalie,

More than anything, I want to tell you from my heart, just how special you are to me, and how much you are loved. Don't ever forget that. You can achieve anything, and you are capable of creating your own happiness. You have made me truly happy and you continue to bring great joy to my life.

You are three wonderfully unique individuals, so much alike yet so different. When all of us are together, we are a family, a single harmonious unit whose different pieces are all working, supporting and sharing for the betterment of each other and 'the whole'.

Life is good - remember that. No matter what happens today, tomorrow will be a better day. Believe it and take it as the truth from me, your father. Find the best in each 'moment' and use your moments to let everyone around you know how much you love them. Remember that this wondrous world of ours is yours for the taking, and especially for the giving. Don't fritter your opportunities away, and don't waste time. It is your most precious resource.

They say God chooses your parents and he gifted you to me; I strive to live up to that challenge. I know at times that I fall short, but you should know that I do the very best I can and I always will for you. Know that you are my life's work and nothing is more important to me than every moment we spend together. Your mom and I are here to protect you as best we can, and to enable you to grow up to be confident, happy individuals. Your mother and I will always try our best and will always love you.

Remember to follow your own dreams and your own lives; you are not responsible for your mom's and my happiness. Never feel uncomfortable or odd for choosing your own path. You will make us proud of your courage should you take the path less travelled, if that is your goal. Our dreams and insecurities are ours, and ours alone. We have faith that you will each create fulfilling and happy lives, but no matter what you do, we love you and our home is always your home.

Your lives stretch ahead of you into a future with lots of opportunities. It's OK to try new things and realize they don't work for you. It's OK to take chances, to fall. But remember to get up, learn what tripped you, and then to move on with confidence. Half of life is just about 'showing up' and having the courage to move forward. You can achieve whatever you set your mind to.

Be generous, and never forget how fortunate you are. Understand your actions have consequences, both for others as well as for yourselves. Our responsibility to make the world a better place starts with you, even in something as simple as saying hello and smiling to someone who is sad or by themselves. Don't worry about the number of friends you have -be more concerned with the quality of them. When the kid on the playground gets bullied, stop the bullies—that kid could be you. The smallest of kindnesses can have the most profound impact on someone in need.

Distance yourself from those who treat you badly; negative energy is a drain. Embrace change. Change is good, it allows us to grow. Don't be afraid of it, welcome it. The only thing you can be assured of in life is that things will change. When you accept that, it seems almost pointless to be afraid of it.

Be yourself, but be your "best self" - a unique individual and understand that you are part of a greater community and respect that. But never follow blindly - be curious about everything and ask questions, even about religion. Stop to ask why and if it doesn't sound right to you, keep inquiring until you get to the answer that sits well with You!! And then be ready to shift that when or if you hear a better answer.

My life is better than I ever imagined it would be and you have made it even richer. I love the three of you with all my heart. And though I would do anything for you, your lives are yours to live independently.

Give back and volunteer. You will have more choices than we had, and will hopefully make fewer mistakes. However, remember it is because of other's generosity that we are all here.

Lead a balanced life. Friends are important to your wellbeing. Your health is important and finding a passion and love for something is important. Get a hobby, travel and experience the world. Whenever I have chosen an experience in the past, the benefits paid me back three or more times the cost. Don't worry too much about the money; it comes and goes.

Save some, donate some and enjoy. When we make mistakes, we learn and grow; this is a good thing. Like playing chess, play the game out to the last move. Sometimes it is in the last moves where the tides of change occur, and the tables turn. Like life, you need to be there the whole time. Often when things seem the toughest, change occurs.

A final thought I want to share with you is that life is a journey, and I am here to be a guide. I am always willing to chat, share and be there for you when you need me. I want you to know how special you are to me and that I hope we will share these ideas together over time. If some days I am too tired or don't make the time, I am sorry because in my heart, I am excited to hear about your lives, your dreams, and your wishes and love nothing more than when you share them with me.

I love you.
Your daddy

The Letter that Started This Book

- Rabbi Lord Johnathan Sacks

Dear Sara, Dear David,

I am writing these letters to you as Yom Kippur approaches, because it's the day on when we ask the deepest questions about our lives. Who are we? How shall we live? What chapter will we write in the Book of Life?

It's also a time to say the things we've left unsaid. The most important thing your mother and I want to say is that you are our beloved children. You have given us more joy than you can ever know. In all of life, you were God's most precious gift to us.

Perhaps there were times when we said things to you, or you to us, which we later regretted. Please wipe them from your memories. God forgives us: let us forgive one another. Life is too short for anger or anguish. Now you have both married and become parents. May your children give you the joy you gave us.

What inspired me to write these letters is the old Jewish custom that parents write their children Tzavaot, "ethical wills." It's based on the idea that the most important legacy we can give our children is not money or possessions, but spiritual ideals.

I truly believe that give your children too much money or material gifts and you will spoil them. They will grow up unhappy and unfulfilled, and in the long run they won't thank you. It will damage them and your relationship with them. Tradition was right. The best things any of us can give our children are values to live by, ideals to aspire to, an identity so that they know who they are, and a religious and moral heritage to guide them through the wilderness of time.

Children grow to fill the space we create for them, and if it's big, they will walk tall. Ideals are big; material possessions are small. Ideals are what make life meaningful. People may envy others for what they earn or own, but they admire others for what they are and what principles they live by – and it's better to be admired than to be envied.

That is what Yom Kippur is about. Judaism sets the bar high. It's a demanding, challenging religion, but that is its greatness. If I were to define what it is to be a Jew; I would say it is to be an ambassador for God.

We were never asked to convert the world, but we were asked to be living role models of justice, compassion, Chessed and Tzedakah. We are the people of the Book, who put learning and study at the pinnacle of our values, to show that faith is neither ignorant nor blind. We were asked to live our faith, day-by-day, act-by-act, through the complex choreography we call halakhah, the intricate beauty of Jewish law. Judaism is a religion of high ideals translated into simple daily deeds.

That's what we received from our parents. It's what we have tried to give you. It's what we hope you will give your children. Not expensive clothes or holidays or the latest mobile phone. These are distractions from life, not life itself.

Life is made by what you live for.

I say this to you at this holy time because I've seen too many people make the same mistake. Their marriages fail or they have a breakdown in relationship with their children and they ask, "What did I do wrong? I gave them everything." True, but not true. They gave them everything except what mattered: time, attention, selfless respect, and genuine, ethically demanding, spiritually challenging values.

Ideals will bring happiness to you and your children.

Life's too full of blessings to waste time and attention on artificial substitutes. Live, give, forgive, celebrate and praise: these are still the best ways of making a blessing over life, thereby turning life into a blessing.

Sara, David, our beloved children: you will never know how many blessings you have given your mother and me. The best we can give you is to pray that God help you to be a blessing to others. Be the best you can, be an ambassador for Judaism and the Jewish people, use each day to do something demanding, and never be afraid to learn and grow.

We love you. May God write you and your children in the Book of Life.

Chapter 1

A Bundle Of Dreams

Every parent wishes only the best for their children. This is a universal phenomenon. It's hard-wired into our very nature. We all want our children to have full, rich and meaningful lives. As finite beings, we enjoy the fact that our children can continue where we left off. We wrap the hopes we have for our children in a careful bundle – a bundle of dreams.

As our family trees grow and expand, each new precious off-shoot deserves special care and protection. It's a beautiful thing to see in action.

As you read through these letters, you will notice the many dreams that these parents cherish. Some are more realistic than others. Some set their hopes high, while others are more forgiving. What is common through all of them is the dream. The next letter from W.E.B. Du Bois to his daughter is a charming expression of this common sentiment. In the letters that follow, you will notice the same theme echoed in many different ways. One has the point of view turned upside down. Another relates some quirky family behavior, and one expresses the unique situation of a modern family. Each one is carefully bundled in its own way.

From the moment we know that we will become parents, our way of thinking about our own world changes, expands and matures. What could be more important than passing on the lessons we have learned, and letting our kids know how we feel?

Sound Advice

– W. E. B. Du Bois

This beautiful letter was written by activist and author W. E. B. Du Bois to his 14-year-old daughter, Yolande. The letter was written when she left home in 1914 to study at Bedales School in England.

Dear Little Daughter:

I have waited for you to get well settled before writing. By this time I hope some of the strangeness has worn off and that my little girl is working hard and regularly.

Of course, everything is new and unusual. You miss the newness and smartness of America. Gradually, however, you are going to sense the beauty of the old world: its calm and eternity and you will grow to love it.

Above all remember, dear, that you have a great opportunity. You are in one of the world's best schools, in one of the world's greatest modern empires. Millions of boys and girls all over this world would give almost anything they possess to be where you are. You are there by no desert or merit of yours, but only by lucky chance.

Deserve it, then. Study, do your work. Be honest, frank and fearless and get some grasp of the real values of life. You will meet, of course, curious little annoyances. People will wonder at your dear brown and the sweet crinkly hair. But that simply is of no importance and will soon be forgotten. Remember that most folk laugh at anything unusual, whether it is beautiful, fine or not. You, however, must not laugh at yourself. You must know that brown is as pretty as white or prettier and crinkly hair as straight even though it is harder to comb. The main thing is the YOU beneath the clothes and skin—the ability to do, the will to conquer, the determination to understand and know this great, wonderful, curious world. Don't shrink from new experiences and custom. Take the cold bath bravely. Enter into the spirit of your big bedroom. Enjoy what is and not pine for what is not. Read some good, heavy, serious books just for discipline: Take yourself in hand

and master yourself. Make yourself do unpleasant things, so as to gain the upper hand of your soul.

Above all remember: your father loves you and believes in you and expects you to be a wonderful woman.

I shall write each week and expect a weekly letter from you.

Lovingly yours,

Papa

Tell Me How

– Daniel Meyerov

Eden and Alex,

I am going to be the best dad to you that I possibly can.

To accomplish that, I've written ideas down as if you two were telling me how to act, so that you will grow up healthy and happy.

1. How you love, respect and believe in me is how I will love, respect and believe in myself.

2. Ask how I am feeling, and then take the time to really listen to my answer. I need to know that my voice counts.

3. I learn how I should be treated and loved, by how you treat and love my mom, whether you are married to her or not.

4. If you are angry with me, I feel it even if I don't understand it. So talk to me and explain.

5. Every time you show grace, kindness and compassion to me or someone else, I learn to trust God a little more.

6. I need to experience your physical strength as a nurturing, protective and safe energy, so that I can learn to trust the physicality of men.

7. Please don't talk about sex like a teenage boy when I am around. It will make me think it is something dirty.

8. When your tone is gentle and your focus is on me, I understand what you are saying much better.

9. How you talk about female bodies when you're 'just joking' is what I will believe about my own.

10. How you handle and care for my heart is how I will expect it to be cared for by others.

11. If you encourage me to find what brings joy, hope and meaning to life, I will always seek those things.

12. If you teach me what 'safe' feels like when I'm with you, I will know better how to guard myself from people who are not.

13. Teach me a love of art, science, and nature, and I will learn that my intellect, my heart and my soul matter.

14. Let me speak my mind, even if you think it's silly or wrong, and then take the time to discuss it with me, because I need to know that my having a strong voice is something you admire.

15. When I get older, if you seem afraid or uncomfortable with my changing body, I will believe something is wrong with it.

16. If you live passionately and embrace dreams, love and contentment for yourself, so will I.

17. When I ask you to let go, please remain available—I will always come back and need you if you do.

18. When you demonstrate tenderness, emotion and compassion, I learn to embrace my own vulnerability rather than fearing it.

19. When you let me help fix the car, paint the house and carry the groceries, I will believe I can do anything a boy can do, and that I have no limitations.

20. Please don't lie, because I believe what you say.

21. Don't avoid having hard conversations with me, because I am smart enough to understand.

22. When you live responsibly and you do everything you can to take care of your family, you teach me how to be self-reliant.

23. If you show me how much my grandparents mean to you, you show me how much you will mean to me and my children.

24. Even though I sometimes may say differently, I need you to be my daddy more than I need you to be my friend.

25. You will be my hero always, and in my eyes, you have hung the moon.

With every day that passes, I see how nothing else matters but you two, Eden and Alex.

Love,
Dad

Grandpa is Eager to Learn from You

- Joel Gusman

Dear Lorenzo,

I am writing to you while you are at an age too young to read, but it is my hope and expectation that the time will come soon when you will be capable of understanding them.

Sharing with you these thoughts and emotions today is only the beginning of what I am anticipating to be an open, honest, loving, fun– filled grandson/grandfather relationship.

First off, you should know and appreciate the fact that you have come into this world amidst lucky and fortunate circumstances. Your Mother and Father love each other deeply and are ready, willing and able to give you almost everything one might need to lead a rich, fulfilling life. Your extended family (great grandfather, grandparents, aunts and uncles) provides similarly wonderful surroundings for you; a world I am confident you will enjoy and cherish.

So, I am happy for you that whatever takes place in the future or wherever your path turns, you had a great head start. Not everyone does.

Will you make the most of this gift? I don't know, but I am so encouraged by what you've shown us in your first 8 months (here's a list – it's not a complete list for sure):

You connect personally eye–to–eye with those in your field of vision. You enthusiastically recognize those whom you have seen more often. You smile brightly and frequently to those around you, to let them know that you are happy and appreciative of their attention.

You only complain (cry) when something needs "fixing" (for example hunger, tiredness, diaper change).

You are comfortably flexible in being moved from person–to–person and place–to–place.

You laugh outwardly with authenticity when your internal sense of humor is poked.

You can spend much time sitting by yourself peacefully and playfully exploring your surroundings while attempting to master your newfound abilities.

You seem to be acknowledging and understanding both English and Spanish languages.

You are particularly entertained by musical toys, which may indicate audiophile interest or talent.

You are naturally lovable with an attractiveness and magnetism that reaches out with friendliness.

To be honest, I am surprised to have such a strong awareness of you and affection for you after only eight months. Our time together rarely exceeds a few hours a week.

Yet, I know the love I am feeling comes directly from WHO YOU ARE already and perhaps even from my sense of whom you will be. You are a boy who I will like to get to know, and one with whom I will love to share experiences. Even better, I am your Grandfather; a title I embrace with pride, respect, responsibility and gratitude.

As such, I look forward to us being great friends. I happen to have lived a great many more days than you, so I feel I can offer some help and insight along the way.

But keep in mind that it's only been eight months since I have been a grandfather—YOUR Grandfather—so you still have so much to teach me…please…I can't wait!

So, best of luck ahead. I think you will deserve it. You are truly loved. I am there for you always.

Love,
JoJo

The Day You Were Born

- Eric Schreiber

To our dear Jacob, Shayna and Evie,

We wanted to write you this letter to let you know how much we love you and to give you some advice going forward with your lives. Each one of you has blessed our lives and made it special in your own unique way.

Jacob, we will never forget the day you were born. It was quite a surprise that, with mom having been in labor for the entire night, that you were about to be born by an emergency C–section. Dad will never forget the doctor throwing him a pair of scrubs and saying you were going to meet the world in just a few minutes. Then, you were born, wide-eyed ready to take in your world. It was not surprising that this quality has stayed with you your entire life. You have always been inquisitive, interested in how things work and why we do the things we do. This has carried over to your academic career, where you have never stopped questioning the world in which you live. In the meantime, you have become an excellent student, a top notch athlete, and a kind person well–liked by your friends, teachers, and, of course, your family.

Shayna, you were the first girl born into our family in over 40 years, and, let's just say, you were worth the wait. You possess rare qualities, including the ability to step in front of crowds of people, not worrying at all about what they think. I can remember when you were only five years old, yet captivated the entire school with your magic act at the talent show. You also have a wonderful sense of humor and a true sense of wonder at what the world has to offer. But, more important is your kind sense of caring. You truly care deeply about the feelings of others and do nice things to help better their lives. Never give up your confidence, sense of wonder, and, especially your innate ability to make the lives of others better.

Evie, our youngest. We will never forget the day you were born. Even though you were a planned c– section, imagine our surprise when the doctor told us you were going to be born three weeks prior to your scheduled date. Up and until you were born, dad and grandpa had gone to fifteen straight Dodger opening day games together. As it turns out, that streak was about to be broken. Even though that game was the first and only time a Dodger hit for the cycle at Dodger Stadium, dad and grandpa didn't mind missing it because we got to meet you for the first time. Your smile and sense of humor makes every day better. Your love for your family cannot be matched, and we are so very proud of you.

It is true, you have been blessed with wonderful gifts. But, having ability is not what makes you who you are, it is what you do with them that makes you a truly great person. If there are two things we want you to take away from this letter it is: 1. Always use your gifts and talents to the best of your abilities to help others and make the world a better place; and 2. Always remember that no matter what happens in this life, you will always have each other. As you grow and develop, and learn new and different skills, always think how you can use your gifts and talents to help others. Most importantly, remember that mom and dad are extremely proud of you and that we will always love you more than anything.

Love,
Mom and Dad.

Tools to Navigate This Life

– Amy Scher Spurlin

To my dearest blonde and my feisty redhead:

Several months ago I attended a management conference where we did an exercise called the Two Minute Drill. The premise of the exercise was that we were about to die, and had only two minutes to write a letter to someone to express what we wanted them to know about life. I chose the two of you. Here's what I wrote then:

Know how loved and special you are. Be true to yourself. Laugh often. Forgive, both yourself and others. Don't judge. Be humble. Put yourself in someone else's shoes. Love big. Love hard. Take risks. Speak your mind.

Two minutes wasn't nearly enough time to tell you all I want you both to know about this world. Life is precious, and every day we are reminded at how fragile it is. The years have passed so quickly since you were babies, when every moment offered an opportunity to learn a new skill or have a new adventure. My wish for you as you continue to grow into young adults and on into adulthood is that you keep that sense of wonder.

Quite often as adults, we get so wrapped up in the daily activity of life, taking care of you and following the track we think we're supposed to follow toward "success" that we forget the simple joys. It's easy to do that if you don't have your heart open to the world around you. I have done plenty of that myself. The truth is, parents make mistakes just like kids do; some of them more than others. But the good thing about making mistakes is that it helps you to learn. That doesn't mean that the situation always has a happy ending or the lesson learned isn't a painful one. With every experience you have, you will learn a little more about life and a little more about yourself.

And while I don't profess by any means to know all of the answers to life's questions, there are some things I have learned along my journey that will help you navigate your path:

Know how loved and special you are. Not just to me, but by your friends, your classmates, your family, and most of all by God. If you ever feel hopeless or out of sorts for any reason, you can always call on God in whatever manner suits your heart. If you remember that, you will never be alone.

Be true to yourself. I have worked hard to help both of you be self-aware. Even when you were learning how to navigate playground politics in pre-school, I encouraged you to form your own opinions and do what you felt was best. The older you get, the more outside influences will threaten to sway you in one direction or another. Although your peers may not always agree with your decisions, the true friends will respect your heart's choices and you'll shine.

Laugh often. This doesn't mean laugh at the expense of others, but keep a sense of levity about you. As horrible as a situation is, you can almost always find some thread of humor in it. And laughter is the best medicine for a reason – it takes you outside yourself for a moment, gets those endorphins going and just plain makes you happy.

Forgive, both yourself and others. This is one of the hardest things to learn, and it will never be easy. People will hurt you, break your heart, ruin your day and make you feel like you couldn't possibly go on sometimes. But the truth is that holding on to anger and blame, no matter how justified it may be only hurts you. The other person isn't affected in the scheme of things by your unwillingness to forgive, and the longer you hold onto it the more power they have over you. And you need to forgive yourself too. You're gonna screw lots of stuff up, but you can't grow if you're busy holding a grudge against yourself. You deserve to be let off the hook too.

Don't judge. It's too easy to make assumptions and react without having all the facts. You may quite often find that your interpretation of a situation is much different than the intent behind it. You never know what someone else is going through, so get more information first before jumping to con-clusions.

Be humble. Everyone has unique gifts and talents and you are no better than anyone else. It doesn't matter how much material success you have or whether you own the newest and best whatever, it's what's inside that counts. Be the kind of person who treats the CEO and the homeless man the same.

Put yourself in someone else's shoes. Before you decide that you're right about a fight with a friend or you're annoyed because you were asked to do the laundry for the 10th time; be in tune with where the other person might be coming from. You will be able to problem solve so much better if you can see both sides.

Love big. Love hard. You both came into existence because of a great love. Your father and I loved you both before we even met you and so did

God. You will probably love several times in your lifetime, and that's okay. Enjoy them all, and don't hold back. If you keep your heart guarded you will miss out on one of the most amazing things life has to offer. But also know that love can change, and every experience is brought to you so that you can learn something from it. Be open to the message, but don't sacrifice who you are for the sake of love.

Take risks. Life is never going to be easy all the time, and you will encounter situations that terrify you and fill you with doubt. The trick is to feel the fear, and do it anyway. Sometimes the greatest rewards come from taking risks. Don't let fear hold you back from accomplishing what you dream – you can do anything you set your mind and intention to.

Speak your mind. This doesn't mean being outspoken or combative all the time, but rather making sure your voice is heard. Sometimes it will need to be subtle and sometimes it will need to be forceful. Never let anyone steal your voice.

You two, my beautiful blonde and my fireball redhead, are the best things I have ever done. Nothing else compares to watching the two of you find your own way and grow into such amazing souls. I hope I have given you the tools to navigate this life with your head held high and your hearts in tune with the world around you. You have a whole world just waiting for you to conquer.

All my love,
Mom

Blessings From Sister Mary Evelyn Flynn

(Of the Sisters of St. Joseph of Carondelet)

Dear Jameson, Natalie and Flynn,

How blessed you are to be born into a loving family, full of interest and protection.

What do I want for each of you?

A great love of learning – which will take different forms for each of you. Enjoy reading – for information, direction and enjoyment.

Interest in others' accomplishments as well as your own.

An appreciation of art, color, form – beauty in art, music, dance and drama.

Overall, a love of God and the universe in which we live. May your lives be full, happy and satisfying!

Blessings on each of you. With love and prayers,

Aunt Anne Flynn

I Marvel at All You Are

– Barry Levy

My Dear Son,

Writing is often times the only way I know how to express how I feel, so forgive my ramblings—I know of no other way to find the words to express what I feel at this moment.

From the day you were born until this very day, I have marveled at you. I don't use that word lightly: marvel. I marvel at you.

You have such strength, such resilience. At times your siblings can be tough, but it strikes me that watching you persevere seems like the very essence of who you have always been. My boy, you always have persevered. You have always found a way. And it hasn't always been easy.

I know things scare you from time to time, but here's what I marvel at – even the things that scare you, never beat you. Please never lose that quality because it will serve you well.

Recently, a friend of mine asked me to write a letter to my child about what it means to be his or her father. The truth is it's easier said than done. We, you and I, never had that moment where I thought to myself, "Wow, this kid is going to need me to do something to protect him." If anything, it strikes me that my job as your father is to protect the world from you, not the other way around :)

It's not like you were operating heavy machinery at six months, but you have a trajectory and a course that no obstacle seems to throw you off of.

This has been true since your birth. Your delivery may have seemed like business as usual for the doctor, but it didn't look that way from where I was standing. Watching the umbilical cord wrap itself around your neck, while you struggled to push forward – it's like that has never stopped. It's like you have never stopped.

There has never been a challenge too great for you. So I suppose as a father, it has meant that there have been moments when I've been allowed to just marvel. To stand back and just watch in awe; my God, this kid is incredible.

See, with your siblings, it wasn't exactly the same. They came into this world so young. So early. That, quite literally, from the moment they were born, I saw what was needed for me to provide. One of them wasn't even 6 hours old and a nurse practitioner stood between me and what I felt they needed. And in that moment it was all clear. This was my kid. Mine. And there was no way I was going allow anyone to ignore their needs.

Ever.

Today as your father, I need to step in. You are my son. I will not allow anyone to treat you with disrespect or disregard. I will not allow anyone to harm you.

Here's my promise to you. I will always have your back. I will always be there for you.

You may not always know what I've done or what I'm doing or what I'm thinking... maybe sometimes it will be in the background, but please never forget I'm there.

Always.

That is my promise to you. My son.

Love always,

Your father.

Now That It's Time for You to Come

– Jasmine Kosovich

Dear Little Monchichi,

Since you're not born yet —we've got 2 ½ months to go—and since I haven't decided on a name for you yet, Little Monchichi is what John and I are calling you these days.

And the reason for that is that we have a baby photo of your baby mama in which she looks like a cute lil' Monchichi doll!

Monchichi dolls were big in the 80's.

Now try getting that song out of your head!

The woman we're calling your baby mama is the woman whose egg is making it possible for you to be. The woman donated her egg and is your biological mother.

Because, by the time everything lined up for you to come into the world, I was —still am—45 years old, and my eggs weren't up to snuff anymore.

I also decided to have you before I met John, so you have a baby daddy too. Which is to say, there is a man, other than John, who is making it possible for you to be, because he donated his sperm, and he is your biological father.

I haven't met him, though I have met your baby mama a couple of times, and John took our picture, for posterity. I'll show it to you when you're old enough to understand this whole situation.

I also have a baby picture of your baby daddy/sperm donor and 11 minutes of audio, in which he's being interviewed by someone from the sperm bank. He sounds really cool! I'll play it for you too, when you're old enough to understand all of this.

When you see the photo of me and your baby mama/egg donor, you'll see that she and I don't look alike. Some women choose egg donors that look like them, I chose her because I just liked who she was. I don't look like your baby daddy/sperm donor either—and neither does John.

I don't care if you and I look alike or not and I won't ever pretend that you came into the world in any way except the way you did. I won't ever pretend that you are biologically my daughter, though you are, and always will, be my true beloved daughter. I won't pretend anything else because I am so grateful and happy to have you, whichever way you came to be.

And here's another thing that is so wonderful and cool about your baby mama/egg donor and your baby daddy/sperm donor: if you want to meet them when you turn 18 years old, you can.

This arrangement is rare these days, and I'm really happy that you have that option, if you want it.

I tried to have you earlier in my life but you weren't ready to come down.

I know, that last sentence really puts the woo in woo woo. But it's what I really think.

I think that you, your soul, your spirit, whatever you want to call it – was somewhere else (I have no idea where, but not here on earth!), standing by for just the right time to come here.

And you really knew just when to come because this is the best time ever: I'm so ready; we have John with us; we also have Jemma too, your soon–to–be big half–sister; you'll get to spend time with your grandma and grandpa... You REALLY have great timing, little one!

I already love you so much. I can't wait to see you, hear you, hold you, get to know you and love you on a whole other level.

Love,
Mom

Rise to the challenge

Kirsten FV Binder

Dear Faith, Zoe, Laura & Tess,

Growing up, I didn't think I wanted to be a mother. I am so glad that life took me down a different path, because you're the most wonderful people I've ever had the honor to know. I'm so proud and humbled to be your Mommy. It is my greatest hope that things I do and the way I live influence your lives in the most positive way possible.

So why didn't I think I'd want this job—to be this person? Simple: I saw the kind of dedication, patience, and sacrifice it took for my parents to parent me, and I didn't think I could do nearly as well. Fear of failing almost kept me from the single most rewarding experience of my life.

Motherhood scared me, not because I didn't think I was up to the challenge, but because anything less than success was an unacceptable outcome. Two realizations got me past my fear. This first is this: The only way to get to success is by failing. Failing a lot, actually. It's the only way to learn. If you're not failing often, you're not challenging yourself enough—and what kind of life is that? I haven't done everything right as a Mommy, but if you four are any proof, I'm not getting it wrong all the time, either.

The second realization was that I wouldn't have to parent alone. For a whole host of reasons, I never really dreamed of getting married, but meeting Daddy changed all that. Nothing ever felt as sure or worth holding onto as this relationship, once I figured out how well-suited we are for each other. That didn't happen right away, to be honest. On the surface, Daddy and I are not an obvious match. Our relationship works because of how whole we are together. While I see possibility, he sees practicality. I see big picture; he sees details. I'm vision; he's logistics. We butt heads, yet we respect the other's point of view. We challenge each other to keep reconsidering our opinions, keep fortifying our convictions, and keep growing throughout life. As a result, Daddy's dreamier than he was when we met, and I'm certainly more grounded.

The seemingly contradictory messages of "Play it safe" and "Go after your dreams" can, should, and must coexist. Populate your life with people who believe both of these things, not just one or the other. Playing it safe does not mean sitting back, and it definitely doesn't mean taking any shortcuts; it means taking considerate, well-reasoned action. Pursuing your dreams does not mean doing so impetuously; it means doing so with a strategic, long-range plan. The only thing harder than failure is regret, and just as much regret comes from brash and stubborn acts as it does from cowardly inaction.

So trust in your dreams, trust in your plan, and trust in the people who love you—especially when nothing seems to be going your way. That is faith. Having faith lets you embrace the uncertainty and the chaos, if you can believe it. Faith is trusting that what seems like chaos actually exists for a reason, even when that reason is murky, revolting, or just unfathomable. It also means that, even though humans are flawed, evil is real, and our lives are finite, we must always soldier on.

You'll be able to do this, so long as your dreams and your character—what comprise your life's mission—are about fostering joy, hope, and abundance in this world, particularly for those who lack these gifts. The only reason we're here is to counteract the forces bent on bringing about the opposite: sorrow, despair, and poverty in all its forms—physical, intellectual, and spiritual.

If you do everything I've suggested in this letter, you will have a good life. You will also fail, sooner or later. I hope you do. Yes, you read that correctly. If you fail, it'll mean that you're pushing your perceived boundaries, charting new territory, making new discoveries, and forging real progress.

You have to have some stability in your life if you dare to accomplish great things, but stability is not the ultimate goal. Do only what is necessary to establish enough equilibrium in your life to stand on your own two feet. From there, climb. Shift your equilibrium forward. Rise to the challenge. Strategize. Generate momentum. Conquer... or fall short.

Either way, celebrate. Either way, be humble. Either way, assess the world from your new vantage point. Reestablish your equilibrium, and then begin to rise again. Whether you continue on the path ahead or change direction is entirely up to you. And while I want you to proceed with urgency, do not proceed with haste. Speed does not matter. Just keep going, and know that the mindful, purposeful, and righteous path will always be obvious. It will probably be harder than the other paths, but it will be obvious.

I'm prouder of each of you than I can possibly describe, but I can sum up my feelings in three words: Voice, Vocabulary, and Volition. For as different as you are from one another, you are all strong, determined, articulate,

36

creative, and empathetic—everything I ever could hope for and so much more. We lead busy lives that aren't easy all the time, and that's a good thing! Thank you for sticking with us and each other through the hard days, trusting your family to help you get through the rocky moments, and sharing your joy and love along the way. You will do great things in this world. I can't wait to see what they turn out to be.

Love,
Mommy

Face Your Failures, Fears, and Feelings

– Amy Hanlon-Rodemich

To my baby,

I know you are a "big girl" now, but you will always be my baby, no matter how old. As I sit here writing, you are in the next room watching the Care Bears and so, so happy. Life is an adventure to you and full of wonder. My greatest hope for you is to keep that joy and wonder for your whole life.

Life will beat you up on occasion, of that there is no doubt. There isn't a thing I can do to stop it, no matter how much I wish. My advice to you is to feel the pain, let it sink in and learn the lesson, then let it go. There is nothing you cannot overcome or accept.

This may sound strange but I wish for you to fail and fail hard. The greatest development comes from failure, not success. Your mom has learned and grown more from failures and it has made me a better leader, a more thoughtful person and, I hope, a better mommy.

I hope that you will get your heart broken so that you know what it feels like and will use that lesson to treat others with compassion. Hearts get broken and it feels awful, but years later you will have trouble remembering and will laugh.

I hope that you learn the value of money and the importance of saving for a rainy day.

I hope that you are cautious but brave. Never let fear keep you from trying something new, but trust your instincts. If you have a bad feeling, walk away.

Even though you are blessed with good looks, don't dwell on that. Looks fade and you are too smart to let them guide your way. Focus on your smarts, of which you have many. Shoot for the moon but find something that makes you happy, not anyone else.

Don't ever let the fact that you are a girl stop you. Girls are just as capable as boys and don't let anyone ever tell you different.

Always be kind to animals, children and old people. Never look away when you see a homeless person. Stop and say hello and offer a kind word, if you can't offer food or some other comfort. Never look away when you see a disabled person either. They are people too and looking for warmth and connections just like you. And never, ever let racism be a part of your life. It makes no sense and shows ignorance. We are all built the same, we just come in different colors with different accents. Take the time to get to know people.

Lastly, remember that your mommy and your daddy love you more than antything in the world, so remember to call and visit when you are older and have your own life. We think about you all the time and it means a lot when you show you care.

Be kind, be brave, be safe, be fair, and be smart.

All my love,
Mommy

The Heart Fairy

– Amy Goldsmith

I have something to confess to you, but I will get to that in a bit.

First, I want to tell you a little something about me that you may not know. I love notes.

I was raised in a home where notes - long or short, were valued. My grandparents and parents used notes as a reminder or a way to communicate love and sometimes even anger. My entire childhood included notes.

When my parents would travel, my older sister, your Aunt Nancy, would make my lunch. She always would put a note in it. I loved receiving her notes that usually wished me a "happy day" or a "delicious lunch" in her beautiful cursive writing. I had always wished my Mom would do it as well, but she left other notes for me.

In my house, important notes were left on the floor - typically in the entryway near the front door or outside our bedroom. Somehow, we wouldn't miss them. However, if left on a table, they were virtually transparent. The notes were usually a greeting, a reminder to do something, or communication about what time someone might be home or when I needed to be ready to leave. My friend's always thought it was so funny that we left notes on the floor. To me, it seemed efficient and rarely did anything slip through the cracks.

Your great grandparents were the same. In fact as they got older, I felt like I was doing hop scotch between their living room and their front door to avoid stepping on their lengthy to do lists. As your Great Grandpa Joe remembered a task he needed to do, instantly there was a note on the ground. I always wondered as he aged, how he was able to maneuver the countless notes and prioritize the tasks.

In my home, sometimes notes were attached to food in the fridge to remind me that an item was to be saved or quickly consumed, as it might be expiring. If my parents went out at night, often there was a sweet note on my pillow saying, "goodnight." Thank you notes also were a big deal in our home. Your Grandma Barbara emphasized that every gift or super kind gesture required a thank you note. With stationery abound, we'd sit and write thank you notes for birthday gifts, holiday gifts, to teachers at the end of the year and so on.

Before texting and email in school, I would pass notes to friends about where to meet on the recess yard, and write about other adolescent gossip. As students we had to be careful of being caught or else the teacher might read the note aloud. Just in case, I tried to avoid embarrassing topics.

Occasionally when I was a teenager, Grandma Barb used lengthy notes to communicate disappointment or not – so - great behavior. It was a way to avoid a shouting match and often reading something in writing, really hit home. I'd get the point.

When Dad and I married, he soon learned about notes on the ground and it became a way we would communicate (before cell phones!). Love notes, lengthy messages in greeting cards and special notes in luggage if we travelled for work became the norm. Dad incorporated my family's note habit.

Then you two beautiful girls came along. As you know, every time I travel for work or go away with Dad for a quick getaway, I leave you each daily morning, lunch and evening notes. I want you to know even when I'm not in front of you, I'm always with you and you're always on my mind. I love you so much and for me, a note is a great way to tell you. It's a gesture. It took time for me to write it, organize it and make it special and it's a small gift I can give you in my absence.

Although I loved my lunch notes from my sister, when it came to your lunches, I have to admit it was hard not to repeat messages. So that's when I came up with the photo–in–the–lunch–note. It's my way of sending a note about a great memory. Each day, unless I'm away and then you get a written note, I've put a photo of you, our family, or your friends to remind you of how special our lives are. I hope they make you smile. I hear many of your friends look forward to seeing the daily lunch photo!

Also, you don't know this, but on every birthday since you were born, I buy a greeting card and write you a note about how you've grown physically, emotionally, academically and developmentally. It's my love letter to you. I figure when you're older and going through old boxes, you'll find the one unopened birthday card and it will be my gift to you.

Perhaps one day we won't have as much money or stuff, but no one can ever take away my love for you. Every day I want you to know how loved you are and notes are a great way for me to reemphasize how much you are wanted, cherished and loved.

Now my confession. In addition to being your Mom, I'm also the "Heart Fairy." I know— you're probably shocked.

Remember those mornings when you awoke to find dozens and dozens of cut out paper hearts starting at your beds, then into the hallway, down the stairs, through another hallway and then taking you to the heart covered breakfast table that often had a little treat or surprise? That was me. I did it. I would stay up at night cutting out and trying to make a special morning for you.

And now there's this note a historical perspective on our family note writing, a confessional, and another love note to you. I hope that you will incorporate note writing into your lives as a way to stay organized, thank people, and communicate to yourself and others.

You both mean the world to me and have made my life complete. I know one day you'll feel this way about your children and hopefully our note writing legacy will continue.

I hope this has hit the right note...

I love you.

Mom
A.k.a. The Heart Fairy

Chapter 2

Shameless Pride

Parents are often unabashedly, shamelessly proud of their children, even for the smallest accomplishment. Starting from the first sonogram, then birth, the first word, the first potty-training success, or the first tentative step — each new milestone swells a parent's heart with pride. Now this might not be totally justified — but who can blame them? There is a simple, natural joy in watching all things grow and develop. As a parent you get to revisit your own childhood - that comes with an automatic sense of wonder. Parents see miracles in the smallest details of their children's development. Some kids go on to become astronauts, like Malcolm Scott Carpenter's son, in the next letter. Others have a more humble, but nevertheless extraordinary destiny. It makes little difference to the parent, in the end. They will be proud. Why not let it be known? Shameless pride is another common theme in many of the letters collected here. Still — children all too often grow up with insecurities and fears, so there's nothing more comforting than a parent's recognition, affection and support.

With all their faults, natural limitations, and oddball idiosyncrasies, our kids are exceptional. It just makes sense to tell them that they are noticed, and that they are worthy.

Discover Mother Nature's Secrets

- Marion Scott Carpenter

Half a century ago, 37-year-old Malcolm Scott Carpenter piloted the Aurora 7 into space, becoming only the second American to orbit the Earth. The day before his landmark journey, he received the following letter from his father, Marion, found in For Spacious Skies: The Uncommon Journey of a Mercury Astronaut.

Dear Son,

Just a few words on the eve of your great adventure for which you have trained yourself and anticipated for so long - to let you know that we all share it with you, vicariously.

As I think I remarked to you at the outset of the space program, you are privileged to share in a pioneering project on a grand scale - in fact the grandest scale yet known to man. And I venture to predict that after all the huzzas have been uttered and the public acclaim is but a memory, you will derive the greatest satisfaction from the serene knowledge that you have discovered new truths.

You can say to yourself: this I saw, this I experienced, this I know to be the truth. This experience is a precious thing; it is known to all researchers, in whatever field of endeavor, who have ventured into the unknown and have discovered new truths.

You are probably aware that I am not a particularly religious person, at least in the sense of embracing any of the numerous formal doctrines. Yet I cannot conceive of a man endowed with intellect, perceiving the ordered universe about him, the glory of the mountain top, the plumage of a tropical bird, the intricate complexity of a protein molecule, the utter and unchanging perfection of a salt crystal, who can deny the existence of some higher power.

Whether he chooses to call it God or Mohammed or Buddha or Torquoise Woman or the Law of Probability matters little. I find myself in my writings frequently calling upon Mother Nature to explain things and citing Her as responsible for the order of the universe. She is a very satisfactory divinity for me. And so I shall call upon Her to watch over you and guard you and, if she so desires, share with you some of Her secrets, which She is usually so ready to share with those who have high purpose.

MoveWith all my love,
Dad

Fail, Apologize, and Be Amazed

- Richard Shapiro

Dear Ashley and Brandon,

We are writing to you on Mother's Day! Your mom and I love you with all of our heart. We want nothing more for you than a long life filled with health, love and happiness!

Your mom and I are in our 40's, and we've discovered a few lessons along the way that we thought we would share with you. The first is truly one of the hardest to learn. We want you to know that failure is necessary! You will try so many things and sometimes fail but you must never give up! Just like the first time down the hardest ski slope in Vermont - it's never easy. Failure is just one of the steps towards success. Embrace it and don't be afraid to look silly in front of others; after all, it's the kids that aren't afraid to fail that have the most fun!

Another thing you will soon realize is that apologies to others are as much for you as they are for the other person. It's important when we make a mistake and hurt someone's feelings (as we all do far too often) that we apologize quickly and sincerely. Remember, an apology that includes the word "but" in it isn't a real one! You then need to forgive yourself. Once you do, just move on and don't repeat the mistake. While hurting others with your words is never a good thing, if you learn from the experience you'll grow as a person.

We can all learn so much from our cute puppy, Cody. I was watching him this morning and thinking more about it. Cody lives each day with amazement and enthusiasm!! He really appreciates the smallest things like fresh snow on the ground in the winter, a car ride to Greenwich Avenue or walks along the Mianus River. He remains extremely loyal, loving and always by our side! Shouldn't we learn some of these great traits from him??

Lastly, Mommy and I are usually right about most of the advice we give you. Since we're older, Mommy and I agree that most of the advice that we got from your grandparents, Papa and Deedee and Bubbie and Zadie, has turned out to be really wise!! Now, we didn't always believe them at the time or even follow their advice. Looking back, we really wish we had!!

Brandon and Ashley, we love you more than you can imagine. Always know that we think about you nearly 24 hours a day and we are super proud of you!!

Love,
Mom and Dad

Admiring the Man You Are Becoming

- Kimberlee Leonard

My Dear Mr. Fish,

Most people look at you and see one serious dude. Even from a very young age, you were always the one who didn't make jokes and often even didn't want to laugh, fearing you might hurt someone's feelings. To me, I always understood the serious brooding and the things you were contemplating in your mind. You've had to deal with a lot at such a young age. You want to make things better.

While I know that the divorce and subsequent years of bopping back and forth was beyond stressful, I will never forget the one-day when you asked for a family meeting, at the ripe old age of 9, between you, your dad and me. How clearly you expressed what was bothering you. Not only that, but you offered solutions in an attempt to make everyone happy. It was clear to me that your time of quiet contemplation wasn't just quiet pain as I had feared, but it was a time of processing feelings and situations.

Your maturity in that moment surpassed both your father and me put together. Humbled? Proud? Um, yeah, both!

Yet, in spite of my pride, I know it wasn't fair that you had to go through that at all. Not long after, things changed, by your design. When they did, you began to smile, giggle, sing and once again be a kid. You in fact, asked for a nickname, Mr. Fish because "fish were always up to something, always playing jokes."

So began a new journey. Yes, you are still my serious guy, always doing the right thing and with serious ambitions. You throw yourself into anything and everything that you find interesting, whether learning a card game, understanding all components of airplanes or somehow landing yourself in a Quantum Mechanics class at the age of 12. Your ambition is impressive, but your ability to find all the right opportunities for success makes my heart giggle.

I know you will achieve many great things. I have all the confidence in you and your dreams of going to Annapolis and being a Naval Aviator. Just know your dreams may change. Life morphs and we mature, as do our dreams and goals. And that is okay too.

You are perfect. I hope you know, no matter what, I do everything with you in my mind and my heart. I'm far from perfect, but I do everything with the best intention of giving you more opportunities and support.

Keep being Mr. Fish, the somewhat serious yet goofy guy who loves learning and understanding. Keep doing good deeds through your projects like Operation: Respect and Honor and the Cadets. You're already a stand-up guy and that will take you far!

Love overflowing for you,
Momma

You Give Me Such "Naches"

- Shelly Billik

My dearest, sweetest, precious Jeremy,

I've composed parts of this letter to you in my head so many times, but I had to write it down in case my emotions get the better part of my composure.

I am so proud of you! I know we hear parents saying these words to their children again and again... and the word pride doesn't even come close to describing the overflow of love from my heart. You give me such "naches." For those of you that don't know that Yiddish word, it translates to "comfort" but it's more than that—it's that feeling that all will be good in your life because you are such an amazing little person.

I see the way that you behave in public—just the right amount of manners and sociability, but also the capacity to be silly and have fun. I see how you are with your friends: caring, sensitive, generous. I see how you handle school – again just the right balance of smarts, studiousness, and excitement for learning, but with a healthy dose of skepticism and questioning. And I've witnessed over the past year how you've approached your Hebrew studies, the Torah, relating with Cantor Judy and your tutor Edith, the amazing way in which you've embraced learning how to read Hebrew. Hebrew! The language that looks like chicken scratch, as dad calls it —and you read it without punctuation in the Torah. I don't know if you realize how remarkable that is. But the fact that you've done all this with willingness, without complaining, even on days when you'd probably rather had been at a friend's baseball game, or doing fantasy football, or just sleeping in on a Sunday morning—that is impressive.

But I have to say that what truly warms my heart, is how you relate to your sister. Yes, sometimes I end up being the referee when you bicker or are playing "let's see who can annoy the other one most." But on the whole you are so thoughtful of Alana, always wanting her to be included, wanting her opinion, and wanting her company. I think of all of our amazing family vacations where you would play for hours, covering your entire bodies in red mud at lake Jocassee, or exploring the river, inner tubing, skiing together, and the hundreds of times we've played games by the fireplace, starting early on with charades where we used to end up rolling with laughter. Even when you were forced to go horseback riding, multiple times —you did it—although reluctantly, and ended up heroically forging rivers in New Zealand, or putting up with crazy horses that tried to wipe you out on trees.

And I love how you are with Ima (my mom). Since you were a baby, every time you saw Ima, you'd jump up and down, flail your hands and say "Ima, Ima, Ima!" As if you hadn't seen her for years. The way you were the first to voluntarily stand up at Ima's 90th birthday 6 months ago, and make a speech in front of 60 or so complete strangers, declaring how Ima is your laughing buddy.

You're relationship with dad is so loving, sweet, and funny all rolled up together. And I love our relationship – how we talk about stuff all the time, we love to eat, and oh, how we laugh!!

I also want to thank you for giving me an appreciation for baseball. Watching you play from the time you were four-years old at Mid Valley, and then five at Encino Little League, you provided a window into a sport (which is so much more) that wasn't a part of my childhood. I knew of working the fields in a kibbutz, or seeing the soldiers with Uzzi's on the bus in Israel. My type of field playing consisted of running around in the woods behind our house, playing with pocket knives and making bonfires. And when I started to experience the fun and excitement of your all-star games, starting with that magical six's year, I got hooked.

I remember when we took a road trip to Irvine and you declared in your sweet little baby voice: "We're staying at hotel? We're like the major leaguers!" And I think I speak for all of us, the team, coaches and parents, when I say that that summer was just incredible. Your team won every tournament that summer. And then you guys did it again the next summer as seven's —amazing!

I also have to thank your friends, your teammates, and their parents for being our extended Encino family. I love the fact that you're friends with the kids you went to kindergarten with at Lanai, despite switching schools several times. We are so happy you're here to celebrate with us.

So I guess I'll finish by telling you my wishes for you, dear Jeremy. I hope that you will always be surrounded by good friends —quality over quantity —as long as it's a lot (as Aba, my dad, used to say). I hope you continue to enrich your mind, your body, and your soul. I hope that you follow your own internal guide as you always have, that Judaism will be your moral compass, that you pursue your passions, and that you are true to yourself. I think that the rest—happiness and success will follow.

I love you forever and for always,
Mommy

Your Baba Will Always Be Here For You
- Bob Kaufman

Dear Kaz, Noah, Mica,

A Few Words From Baba. I love you.

I love you so much that the simple action of writing this letter seems like an insurmountable task to fit into words, what words alone simply cannot convey.

I look at each of you with pride, admiration, and sheer amazement. You are all unique and wonderful and totally full of life, curiosity and intelligence.

Kaz: you are a mensch. Warm, caring, mature, talented, fun and you have an emotional intelligence seldom seen in this world. You are genuine and extremely considerate to all. You also have a talent in elevating the spirits of those around you. As an athlete, you are a specimen. You have incredible raw talent, great intelligence and instincts, and that coupled with your ability to be the ultimate teammate will take you far. I love you, I admire you, and I totally trust your way. You make me so proud with everything that you do, and I am with you every step of the way.

Noah: you are truly one of a kind. Your intelligence, eye for detail and complete understanding of all that happens around you, and all that happens around everyone, allows you to have a perspective unique and more comprehensive than all others. You also are decisive, and have a keen ability to hone in on exactly what you want to accomplish and once that happens, there is no stopping you. You also have a big heart and are full of passion. Please be cognizant and considerate of others on your journey to accomplishing the great things that I know that you will accomplish. I truly get you, I love you, I admire you, and I am always there for you.

Mica: my beautiful little girl. I love your ability to command every situation. You have stood your own ground with your brothers and have developed into a beautiful person—caring, brave, loving, happy, and strong. You are the torchbearer of happy, and as such you lighten up everywhere you go. You possess great leadership tendencies, and your caring nature for others will guide you to do great things and help others. You make me smile every day and I love you more than I could possibly convey. Your Baba will always be here for you.

Kaz, Noah, Mica, the true hero of the family is your mother – Ka– san. She is my best friend and the CEO of the family. She is our pillar of strength, and the best partner I could ever have on a journey through life. We have been together now for 18 years, and I love her more every day. We have a beautiful family and the best kids in the world, and together we are a solid family unit. This is because of your mother. Thank you Naomi for your patience with me, your dedication to the family, and your leadership as the CEO of the house. I love you.

Love,
Your dad, Bob (A.K.A. Baba)

You Completed Our Family

- Bruce and Sharon Gersch

I want to take you back in time to the year, 2000. We had two beautiful daughters, a comfortable home, and a German Shepard. We made it through the diapers, bottles, and sleepless nights. I thought that our family was complete, and to be honest, I was done! I repeatedly told Sharon that the world was designed for families of four. Three children would change everything. We would need a new car, a new house, and move from man to man to zone defense. Fortunately, Sharon did not listen. Does she ever listen?

Hailey, you came into our lives at a time when we thought our family was complete. It is not by accident that you came into our family. Everything that happens in life, happens for a reason. There are no coincidences. Life is not random. There is a master plan. You were the missing link.

The fact is, Hailey, you completed our family.

Today, 12 years later, we stand here with our baby, a Bat Mitzvah. Hailey, you have brought joy to our lives each and every day. We have watched you grow, spread laughter, love and compassion to all those around you.

This occasion makes your mother and I look both backward with fond remembrances, and forward with great hopes for your future. You taught me that being the father to a daughter is the most rewarding job I will ever have.

You are now a young adult, and will begin to take full responsibility for your actions. At times it will seem simple and effortless. At other times it will seem difficult and burdensome. As your parents, we'll always be here to help you find your way.

Many of your friends and relatives are here with us today, and we are grateful that they have taken the time to join us in this celebration. Unfortunately, your grandfather is not physically here with us tonight. He is definitely here in spirit, and I can guarantee you Granpa Bill is sitting next to your Zeyde complaining about the cost of this party.

When writing this speech, we came across a quote that in our eyes summed up your past, present, and future.

"Our children are the living messages we send to a time we will not see."

Standing here today, I'm certain that in you Hailey, we are sending the future the right message.

We love you so very much.

Please raise your glasses, and I would like to propose a toast

To the Bat Mitzvah Hailey, who has a heart that is as pure as gold, and always sees the best in people.

To Sharon, my high school sweetheart, we get better with age!

To Casey, and Nicki, we almost made it through your teen years!

To our wonderful family, this celebration could not be without all of your love and support.

To our fantastic friends, who have become part of our extended family, you have been by our side through good times and difficult times.

We love all of you!

Be the Best You

- Becky Yang O'Malley

Dear Isabel

First, I want you to know that I love you very much and that will never change, no matter what. I am the luckiest mommy in the world to have such an amazing daughter like you. The two best parts of my day are 1) when I wake up in the morning and see your sleepy—eyed and smiling face and 2) when I come from work to be welcomed with your smiles and hugs.

I was so proud of you watching you perform at your kindergarten spring recital today. Even though you are just five years old, I can't believe how much you have grown in the last two years. It has been the best adventure watching you grow, learn and explore. When I line up the photographs of you taken over the last two years, I can really see that you are growing up right before my very eyes. However, there are two things that remain ever constant in your appearance—the sparkle in your eyes and your big and beautiful smile.

Aside from your physical changes, I have also noticed how much you have grown mentally and emotionally. At the beginning of the school year, you were just learning to write the alphabet. Now just ten months later, you are reading, writing and doing arithmetic. I love that you enjoy reading and it is so gratifying to read your fun and creative stories. I'm so envious at how easily you pick up math concepts (and mommy is an accountant!). You are a gifted and amazing artist and my office has become a gallery filled with your wonderful artwork. You have the goofiest sense of humor just like your dad – I love your knock– knock jokes and it's a little unnerving that a five year old understands sarcasm.

I have to admit, you're more stubborn and hard– headed than I ever knew a child could be. This is definitely a trait that I passed on to you. You march to the beat of your own drum and have laser beam focus when you have a goal in mind. This sometimes causes arguments and frustration, how-ever, I know that this tenacity and toughness will be an asset to you as you grow older. You are also so compassionate and your natural gift of empathy is clear to anyone who spends time with you. I know that you will be a kind, supportive and strong big sister to Fiona. Even at almost six months, Fiona is already looking up to you. You will have a very important job of being a role model to your little sister.

I am cheering for you and I will do what I can to help you succeed. My hope is for you to be the best YOU. The most important part of growing up is figuring out who you are. As you learn about the world, I want you to remember to always be the very best you can be and always be proud of yourself.

My life would be empty without you. You make me smile and laugh every day. You make me so proud of you in everything you do. You fill my life with so much joy and love.

I love you with all my heart.
Mommy

Helping Me Redefine "Mother"

- Merav Segall

To my children, Talia and Eitan:

From the moment that you entered my life, I was changed forever, destined to abandon all preconceived notions of the "defined" mother. I simply learned to follow my heart; to love truly and deeply, without condition and without hesitation. I have never loved more completely and I have never felt more whole. While I am here to guide you; introduce you to the world and its intricate subtleties, facilitate your growth physically and emotionally, I often feel that you are my teachers. You aid me to expand my limits of acceptance and help me to evolve into a healthier being.

As you grow in this complex world, as you find your paths and engage in relationships and life around you, be who you are. Talia, be complicated and beautiful, kind and intellectual. This world needs your self– reflection and analytical mind. Eitan, be joyful and generous, engaging and smart. This world needs your gentle soul and unselfish heart.

Allow your inner voices to carry you through times of difficulty and times of bliss. Find the joy in every moment. Embody delight and share it with others. Happiness is contagious. Remember the magic of fairies, always, and carry that rapture with you on your adventures.

As you encounter life's peaks and valleys, find your strength from within. Trust who you are and know where you come from. Be true to yourselves and be genuine with others. Be honest, especially with yourselves. Know your boundaries and do not permit others to infringe upon them. Maintain your values even in the face of adversity.

Be kind. Treasure life's challenges in order to discover who you are more exactly. Learn with an open mind, heart and hand. Nurture nature and you will reap the growth of life and love.

Know that I love you always and with all my heart. I love you regardless, because I love YOU.

Love,
Mom

On to the Olympics

- Jeff Mednick

Today is your lucky day! I have been approached by a kind gentleman who I have known for a few years who is writing a book of endearing letters to their grandchildren. I prefer to respond more directly by telephone or one–on–one conversation. I am a man of few words. I do not always express my feelings, my beliefs, and my emotions directly or indirectly.

Ever since you were a little girl, you have had the dream of going to the Olympics, representing the good old USA in gymnastics. Your mother, my daughter, is doing everything in her power to help you succeed in your dream (I almost forgot your father and brother who are also in your corner).

You are an exceptional young lady, who will succeed in "WHATEVER" direction you wish to travel in life.

I live a long way from you, but I am in your corner every day. Everyone has a dream. This dream you have had since you were in diapers (Ha! Ha!!) is a vivid reality that will be realized with your dedication, hard work, determination and will to succeed. The coaches you have are great. They are behind you 100%. Your mother, along with the other tutors is making sure your schooling is not neglected. You cannot be successful in life unless you are multifaceted in your climb up the ladder of success. You have to be multidimensional in your growth of life. Being successful in your career in gymnastics is nothing unless you complete your educational goals.

Arlene and I are in your corner, backing you all the way up to the top of the ladder of success that leads to the Olympics in Japan in 2020.

Love and affection,
Grandpa Jeff and Arlene.

Chapter 3

Overcoming Obstacles

What could be harder than watching your child suffer? Most parents would gladly change places with their youngsters when life deals out its inevitable knocks. Mom kisses each and every bump and scratch better. Dad threatens to haul out the shotgun when his daughter starts dating – we know all the familiar symptoms of over-protectiveness. Who can blame us? As any sensible person knows, of course, these bumps and scratches have a purpose. Though we try to shield them from bullies, failures at school or on the sports field, or from the death of a beloved pet, these things happen anyway. They serve to prepare us for the realities of adulthood. Often they can be wonderful opportunities to learn.

Parenting styles differ, and some are more like protective hens while others are more like pack leaders; but there's a place for every species. Sometimes it really seems like the universe has conspired to place a child with a particular kind of nature under the protective care of just the right kind of parent. Other times we might wonder how it could ever have happened.

Pain is a teacher. Through the fires of adversity, our young ones learn to be balanced, empathetic human beings. As adults, many of us find it difficult to be honest about our own deepest emotional scars sometimes, but what better way to advise those who need it most? Our experiences mean more to kids than empty words. Isn't it better to tell things the way they are, rather than quote from a book?

You can follow this motif like a golden thread through many of these letters.

What I Wish My Dad Shared

– Shannon Segil

Dearest Jameson, Natalie and Flynn,

I am so grateful your Daddy had this idea for parents to write letters to their children. As you know, my Daddy died when I was five. I would give anything to hear his words of advice, thoughts on life or maybe just see a glimpse of his personality. Hopefully my letter will show you all three.

First of all, I am so proud to have three strong-willed, interesting and fiery children. I can't imagine a worse fate than having to raise a trio of milk toasts. I like to think I have learned a few things from life that may help you along your journey:

Always look people in the eye when speaking and have a firm handshake (especially you, Natalie).

Have confidence in, be attuned to and always listen to your inner voice. It will rarely steer you wrong. And if it does, at least you made an honest mistake.

You can't say you don't like something if you haven't tried it. That goes for broccoli, tennis and high school dances.

Be loyal. It's far more important to have two best friends than to have twenty pals. Best friends always have your back – pals may or may not.

Always be kind to animals. People that aren't are super creepy.

I would rather you scream than bottle all your feelings up, but let's try to find a happy medium. Maybe we can learn that one together.

Always say "I love you," when you leave the house or hang up the phone. You just never know when your time will be up and it's nice to leave your family with those words said.

Find a sport. Play it well. You don't have to be the best, but try your best. It will help you focus and expend all that energy you will have as a teenager.

Be proud of your heritage. Being an Irish Jew is a fabulous combo. Learn to love to read. Don't read only what is assigned by your teachers.

Books can take you places that you never dreamed of.

Know that Mom and Dad will protect you no matter what. We will help you out of any jam – you just have to talk to us.

Understand how lucky you are to have siblings. They were your first best friends. There will come a point in your life when you will understand that family is everything.

Have a friend of the opposite sex. It will help you gain a whole new perspective on life.

Travel as much as possible. Do a semester abroad. Have the courage and just do it. You can run out of time in life and your obligations start adding up. Do it while you can.

Now obviously these aren't all the words of wisdom I hope to bestow upon you, but that's the beauty of Daddy's idea¬¬—I can write as many letters as I want! But the most important thought you can take from this letter is that you are, always have and always will be truly and deeply loved. Nothing and no one can ever change that. Life has its ups and downs, but that eternal love I have for you will always remain. You are my most important accomplishments.

Love,
Mommy

Determination, Hard Work, and Continuous Education

– Larraine and Clive Segil

To our beloved grandsons Jack Jonah Noah and Gabriel: Life Lessons

1. Choose your life partner well - not the perfect one but the one whose potential to grow with you during your lives is clear

As you know Grandma's dream is to dance at all of your weddings since one of the goals I have for you is to find a life partner with whom to share laughter, sorrow, achievement, failure and emotional and physical intimacy. On those four wedding days I pray that what I will dance for, will be for joyful healthy lives for you and your families.

2. Take calculated risks not foolish ones - hedge your bets - don't put everything into one area - spread it around, focus only in a few arena and be expert at those!

Your lives have been so blessed to be born and raised in the USA. That was no accident although you may take your good fortune for granted . Our family history is one of great risk-taking all with the end of providing a better life for our children and future generations.

Your great great grandfather Isaac Wolfowitz and his wife Rebecca fled from Lithuania to South Africa to escape from pogroms by the Russians who killed many jews. They had no money and travelled to Johannesburg. So life began again and soon they had 6 children - 4 girls then a son called Jack and another boy Punny, thereafter . Jack was 14 when his father died and his mother lost the family butcheries to Isaac's brother and all of a sudden their calm middle-class life fell apart. Jack started two music bands which brought in extra money and they scrapped by. That was when Jack decided that he would never be poor again. And he never was. Your great great grandparents on your Zayda's side and his mother Miriam had similar beginnings - coming from Kovna and Lithuania - to establish a life in South Africa settling in Boksburg where Zayda's father Arnold was born and became a family doctor. He married Miriam and together they built a life of philanthropy giving much to the Jewish Community in their town.

I wrote a novel called Belonging in which my parents Jack and Norma Wolfowitz's lives were chronicled - read it if you have not already. Why was 'Belonging' the title ? Because anyone who has left behind the familiar life and circumstance in which they felt comfortable, and dared to reach out and risk everything in a new country where they knew no one - is somebody who for the rest of their lives always needs and wants to BELONG in that new place.

3. Welcome the stranger, help those who do not belong to feel comfortable - since ALL of you DO belong.

My mother's parents also took a big risk - during World War I 1914-1918 my grandfather Harry Cohen was one of the very few Jewish aviators (pilots) in the RAF and he survived that terrible war. The British government gave veterans of that war a resettlement allowance if they would go to South Africa which was then part of the British empire. They went with their two year old daughter, my mother. Harry my Grandpa was a cabinet maker. He started the first furniture factory in South Africa. So just like your daddy, Zayda Clive and your Grandma Larraine he was an entrepreneur. He was one of the first leading industrialists of the 20th century in Southern Africa. He made a beautiful life for my Granny Charlotta and my mother and her brothers.

When your Zayda and I met and married, we went to live in Canada and on our return we decided to leave South Africa forever and come to Los Angeles. Your daddy was two. It was history repeating itself again. Although no one was persecuting us they were persecuting others and we wanted no part of it.

So from a life of wealth in the style of aristocracy we came to America - no money, no contacts, no family and no friends. Just determination, hard work and continuous education.

That is what each of YOU must keep front and center in your lives.

4. No matter how comfortable your circumstance - know that it could all disappear one day - but three qualities - determination, hard work and continuous education - will help you always to land squarely on your feet.

Your daddy learned the ways of America like few people ever do and his success brings me and your Zayda Clive so much joy and fills us with pride

5. Choose your advisors well. Do not be influenced by those who have self-interest as their goal - this is a tough one.

And so my dear Jack, Jonah, Noah and Gabriel, the four of you along with the children of Uncle Anthony and Uncle Clifford are the light of our lives. Zayda and I wanted 6 children but it was not to be. All of you have filled us with joy and love. We thank you for every single glorious moment - wherever you are and regardless of your ages we will be with you in spirit as our love protects and nurtures you.

Grandma Larraine and Zayda Clive

You Are Amazing!

– Brian Shapiro

Alexandra, I know what you're thinking right now, "Dad, I hope you don't talk too long, I hope you don't say anything that will embarrass me and most of all, I hope you don't start to cry!"

Well, tonight I can't make any guarantees. Wow! You made it! I can't believe this day is finally here. We are so proud of you! You made a decision over four years ago to learn more about your Jewish faith and you brought your family along for the experience. This has been an interesting experience for me to watch you go through Hebrew school over the last few years and teach me more about Judaism and some of the traditions that go along with it. I know that you will do very well and be able to handle your new responsibilities going forward as a Bat Mitzvah.

Alexandra, you know that I've had issues watching you become a young woman. In the last year or so, you've started shaving your legs, wearing makeup, texting your friends, including some young men; you want to go to the mall with friends, but you don't want your parents to come along. This is tough.

I remember as if it was yesterday when you were born. You were this warm little bundle that I was so afraid to drop in the delivery room. I wasn't sure I would be able to handle the responsibility of raising children. Your mother assured me that I would do ok. All I knew is that I wanted to be around you all the time.

As I thought of different ways to close this out, I thought of another little story. A few months ago, you took my phone and changed your contact entry to read "Alexandra is amazing" so now when you call me I get to see that. You are amazing! I was going to sing that song, you know the one that says you're amazing just the way you are, but I thought that might be a little embarrassing for you and you might want to vote me out of the bat mitzvah.

I love you, baby. Have the happiest of birthdays!

Love,
Dad

Let Go of Loss & Make Happy Days

– Laine Sigesmund–Eztoni

My Children:

When your father was alive, I was very happy. His love gave me the ultimate happiness, as true love can. After he died, I was broken. Many years have passed and I am happy again, but it's different now. My happiness is different. I am different. Before, I attached my happiness to Michael, now I stand on my own two feet, and I'm happy again, because I realized if I ever wanted to live again, I mean really live, I would need to rebuild myself. I've learned to no longer attach happiness to a person or material things.

Happiness needs to come from within. I'm happy because of me. I'm happy because, after many years of being closed and afraid, I woke up and I became open to experiences and passions that fed my soul. I opened to the journey, to the lessons, to living in the moment, being present, and I opened my eyes to what and who is truly important in my life. Happiness is being free of jealously, of not judging others, or caring about what other people are doing or what they think about me.

I understand now the only person I need to be better than tomorrow is the person I am today.

Happiness is about helping people, being kind, and being generous. It's about having a willingness to be vulnerable, to be open, be a feeling person, saying what you feel needs to be said at that moment, and doing it without fear. It's about not being afraid to love, and knowing if you get hurt you'll still be okay. It's about remembering the joy of the past and letting go of the pain. The wound is still here, it runs deep, but I have learned to live with it and to grow from it, to not let it handicap me, as I allowed for years. I still feel sadness. I don't pretend these feelings aren't there. I honor them and the moment passes. Happiness is about being appreciative of today, and excited about the possibilities of tomorrow. It's not about the big, monumental events, it's about enjoying the beauty and simplicity of the small things. It's the little bits of happiness that add up to greater overall happiness.

In life we have choices. A few years ago I decided to no longer be a victim. I made a conscious decision to empower myself, take control of my life, and overcome my helplessness. Through empowerment I learned to drop some of that pride and learned to ask for help (my pride only hurt me). I asked for help from all kinds of friends, and you know what they did, they obliged, and expected nothing in return. I showed them appreciation and gratitude (and some didn't even expect it!), because your true friends give from the heart, they don't expect anything back. Some didn't think my appreciation and gratitude were enough (I figured out very quickly where I stood with them!). You see, I learned not everyone is rooting for you. Some people will never like you or they will always be jealous of you and enjoy your failures. This is okay. These are the people you don't need to be close with. These people are not your friends. Recognize who they are, and keep these toxic people at a distance. They will never be happy for your successes because they are unhappy with themselves. Our village is made up of our true friends. Be there for them and they will be there for you. When you have your village, you will never be alone.

Humor will help to get you through. Approach everything in life with a sense of humor. If you can't laugh at all the things that go wrong, you're in trouble, because a lot of things go wrong, all the time.

Set boundaries and don't be a people pleaser. If you don't want to do something, just say no. (note: this rule does not apply to your schoolwork xo, Mom). Don't do what you don't really want to, this will just make you resentful, not happy.

Bad things happen to all of us at different times in our lives. We have a lot of disappointments. We all have wounds. We all fail. Try to not let these things destroy you. We can't control when bad things happen, but we can control how we react. When bad things happen I acknowledge what has happened and look for the silver lining. This is where the lesson is. You just need to look for it. It's part of the journey.

As long as you are open to learning from the journey, you can grow from it. Be brave, honor your feelings, be open, empower yourself, be forgiving, try to make good choices, depend on your village for support, look for the silver lining, laugh a lot, and have faith. These things will give you the strength you need to get through the worst times. It's never too late to make your life what it's supposed to be. We only have so many days. You are in charge of making yours happy ones.

My unconditional love always,
Mommy

Figuring Out Who You Are at Age 12

– Chris Yeah

A Letter to Jason on His 12th Birthday

It's hard to believe that it's been 12 years since I became your dad. While I knew that it would change my life, I didn't know how much it would affect both my daily activities and my overall perspective.

I still remember being 11 years old, and wishing I could stay that age forever. Even then, I knew that I would probably never have so carefree an existence again. I dreaded that 12th birthday.

Yet as the calendar shows, I've managed to survive turning 12. And 13. And a lot of other birthdays (though I'm not going to say exactly how many). And as an old man who was once a boy, I wanted to share some advice that I hope you'll be able to use for the rest of your life.

The most important part of growing up is figuring out who you are. You're still learning about the world, and that's fine. That knowledge will come with time. But self– knowledge will only come if you seek it out.

The best way to figure out who you are is to try doing different things. Life is complicated and difficult to imagine without first-hand experience. Go out and get that experience, but do so safely—there's not a lot that risking life and limb teaches you.

No one has the right answers so don't rely on other people to tell you what to do. Even I, in my incredible wisdom, have been known to get things wrong. Seek wise counsel, but make your own decisions.

The best way to learn from others is from their actions, not their words. People are terrible about predicting how they'll feel or what will make them happy. Instead, use the power of surrogacy. Find people who feel or have what you want, and learn from their example.

It's bad to lie to others, but it's disastrous to lie to yourself. I believe that the truth is the best policy (if nothing else, it takes less energy than remembering all your lies) but even if you decide you need to lie to others, never lie to yourself. Either you'll start to believe yourself, or worse, you'll stop believing in yourself.

When in doubt, be kind. There aren't many situations where treating someone badly is the right decision. Even if you need to say no, or thwart someone's desires, being nasty rarely helps you, let alone the other person.

In the words of Abraham Lincoln, "This too, shall pass." Sometimes good things will happen. Sometimes bad things will happen. Sometimes you'll be ecstatic. Sometimes you'll be bitter. Whatever the circumstance, recognize that all things are temporary, and everything changes. That may help you stay calm and grounded.

(There's other advice I'll need to give you in a few years, but let's just leave that for the future, shall we?)

Love,
Dad

My Personal Miracles of 9/11

– Ari Schonbrun

In hindsight, I could probably divide my life into two: Before and After 9/11. September 11, 2001 was the day of my rebirth.

I'd been working at Cantor Fitzgerald for nearly a decade. I had recently been promoted to head of global accounts receivable. Thus I was dealing with clients around the globe who spoke different languages and lived in different time zones. I was normally found in my office at the World Trade Center, Tower One, before 8:30am.

I usually left Cedarhurst, New York at 7am. After prayers at my synagogue, I would catch a commuter rail on the Long Island Rail Road, heading into Manhattan. As I tried to rush out of my house that fateful morning, I glanced at my watch and saw I was running early. Immediately my mind jumped to the countless projects waiting on my desk that I could get a head start on.

"Dad, can you help me fill out my book form?" my eight-year-old interrupted my thoughts.

"Sorry, no time," I mumbled on the run.

"But Dad, the book form is due today," Baruch pleaded. "I wanted to show it to you last night but you came home too late."

My wise wife, principal of a special education department at a large school, saw his distress and wouldn't let me off the hook. "Ari, you're not leaving the house until you help him complete these forms," she said.

When I finally ran out the door, all I felt was annoyance. Now I'll be late to the office and my entire day will be off schedule.

It was those twenty crucial minutes that made all the difference in the world, for had I left my house at 6:40am as scheduled, I would have been in my office on the 101th floor when Flight 11 hit the first tower. No one above the 92nd floor was able to escape alive.

I will save my readers the gory details which have been widely carried by the media. For me personally, before 9/11, I was your average workaholic, "married" to my job and barely involved in the day-to-day life of my family. I'd been focused on getting ahead at work, earning more and more money, enjoying the superficial trappings of life.

After 9/11, I realized how close I had been to losing the most precious part of my life, the ones I love. In the past, I'd hesitated to take off for my children's school functions, class plays or trips. Today I don't think twice. Being there for my wife and children is more important than anything. My daily prayers in synagogue are much deeper and more meaningful now, and I constantly look for opportunities to help others, in small and large ways.

I feel that God gave me a second chance at life with the enormous miracles of that day; I intend to do my best to live up to it.

My Lifelong Dreams, Realized in You

– Martha Mathewson

Ten years ago, I wrote a letter to myself that I designed to be opened on my twenty– fifth birthday. It was a list of 50 things I wanted to do and places I wanted to go before I died. That it was dated for my twenty– fifth year was only one sign of just how fatalistic and depressive my mind was inclined to be in those years…

At the top of the list were three things: 1) to be married and 2) to have a child and 3) to visit Scotland.

The first of these I flirted with briefly in my early twenties, getting myself engaged to a good friend and breaking his heart two years later when I realized marriage was not, and may never be, my destiny in this lifetime.

The third, I experienced one summer in the company of that same good friend, wandering the hills and dales of the northern United Kingdom in a sporty little European car that got "only" 55 mpg, wading toes in a secret pool of clear heilan water in Glencoe - chasing millennia, old phantoms within the pitch black underground labyrinths of Edinborough, tasting the spray of the North Sea under the sinking shadow of a lighthouse at Rattray Head, counting sheep in daylight and pubs by night.

The second of my lifelong dreams, little one, is You. Since I was a child myself, I've had a deep and still craving, like a thirsty throat that no amount of fresh water can stave, to be a Mother. But my Body became my enemy for many years and I gave up on this dream. This is why I call you my Miracle, and why Your life is more precious to me than my own ever was or may ever be again.

When I was a child, unnatural and cruel men hurt me. They hurt my Body, and they left me thinking, even in my earliest years, that my Life was worthless. Again and again through the years, men with self– hatred filled souls and lazy spirits brought me deep physical and soul pain, until finally at the age of twenty-five, rather than embracing the last of my dreams that I had dictated to myself a decade before, I gave up on everything, and I believe I would eventually—sooner than later —give up on my own Life, also.

But one night I had a dream. I dreamed about a blue–eyed boy with a quiet soul and a rowdy spirit who called me Mother. And a few days later, you entered my corner of the Universe and I knew you were there, to stay. I remember thinking with wonder what a terrible responsibility had been laid on my shoulders, and how weak and unready I felt, and yet how ready I am.

Our journey together, You and I, is still barely in its preface. We may have years, decades, a century, or less. All I know is that you are here – and that you tell me in my dreams, often, but not often enough, that you are here to stay. For a little while, for a lifetime, however long You may choose for that to be.

Did the first Mother feel this awed and this afraid I wonder? I feel often, so overwhelmed, everything so new. I feel as if I must be the first Mother—indeed, I am. I am the first Mother and the last, and You are only the beginning of my lifetime of miracles.

We'll talk again soon, You and I.

Until then, All my Love,
Your Mother

Seek the Magic in Life
– Mark Bernsley

Devon,

I know that you know Mommy and I love you. But you really have no idea how much. You can't. Grandma Dot used say: "When you have kids, you will understand [how much we love you]," and I can only repeat those words to you.

You have worked hard to get here. And we are so proud of you, not just for what you've accomplished and continue to accomplish in your studies, whether here or in school, but also for the good and caring person that you are. You are driven to do well, and you do. Right now your life is very structured between school and homework and skating and music and Hebrew school, you have rarely had time to just be a kid. We acknowledge that.

As you get older, you will have more freedom, but you will also take on more and more responsibility for your own life. We will be here to help you and guide you. Please let us. Please trust us. Not because we know all the answers, but because our experience can help you think things through a little differently.

But there is something more important that I'd like you to remember to do. [Are you listening?]: Continually seek the magic in life.

Do you remember when you were very young, and you used to take my ring so that I could chase you around the house to get it back? For those minutes of that game, there was nothing else in the world that mattered but being in that game—and we had so much fun. That was magic.

The magic is out there in everything: in the stars; the rainbows and the sunsets; in music and in birds chirping in the morning; in feeling a breeze blowing against your skin; in understanding something new; in landing your first axle; in each competition you are in; in dreaming and in pursuing your dreams; and in loving and being loved. In every experience of life that you have, and in every experience of life that you can create for others, you can find magic. And as you find and experience more magic, you will be able to create more magic for yourself and for others.

Now not all experiences will generate the same amount of magic for you.

And clearly I'm not saying to do or try everything, as some things are clearly dangerous or otherwise counterproductive. But if you pay attention, you will discover what resonates with you and what doesn't. So pay attention. Listen to your heart, and be honest with yourself. You will find and recognize more magic that way.

Now, in case you didn't notice: in addition to your successes and achievements, you will make mistakes, and you will have failures. We all do. In addition to your joys, you will have sorrows. We all do. I know because you are our child, that you will be hard on yourself here. Try to give yourself a break and NOT judge yourself by your mistakes. Respect yourself. Allow yourself to experience and find the magic in both doing things well, and in making mistakes. You can learn from both; and both are part of life. We can't appreciate the times we consider "good," without having had some of the ones we consider "bad." We pray, of course, that you have more and greater good times. Again, in both good times and not– so– good times, let us help you. And always remember to find the magic.

King Solomon, blessed with the greatest wisdom, wrote that "Whatever you get to do, do it with your strength." That is not so you can get an "A," make us proud, get into a good college, or make more money, although clearly those are good. It's because when you put yourself completely into the experience at hand, you will find the magic in it. Follow that advice and you will experience more magic. Of course, we still want you to get the A's, and go to good schools—but that's because we know that doing those things will present the greatest opportunities for you to have more experiences, to find more magic, and to appreciate the magic more deeply.

You continue to be the greatest source of magic for Mommy and me. We love you and wish you a lifetime of magic.

Love,
Dad

Reflections for a Mitzvah

– Karen Naide

My son celebrated his bar mitzvah on Saturday, May 5, 2012. Phew... I'm still recovering from the weekend, although in a good way. Jared was flawless, and proved to be everything two parents could ever wish for in their children. We are immensely proud.

Part of the bar mitzvah ceremony (for those who have never been to one) is for the parents to speak to their child, and impart some wisdom to help guide them in their future life.

I got the sappy speech. My husband got the clever and funny one. That's how life always seems to be. So, for your reading pleasure, here are our speeches to Jared:

My Speech:

From the moment you arrived on Mother's Day in 1999, you've captivated my heart completely—first with your adorable face, then with your charm which (believe it or not) was very obvious from the time you were an infant, and then with your kindness, sensitivity, generosity, polite manners and thoughtfulness—traits that are obvious to everybody who meets you.

One of the most formative moments in our lives occurred on October 18, 2005 when you fell from your bunk bed and we ended up at Children's Healthcare for a week with a traumatic injury to your arm. That first day in the ER, the doctors told us they were just trying to save your arm. How could any of us have known in that darkest of moments that this event would shape you into the incredible young man standing before me today?

Over the years, your dad and I watched you take that awful injury and use it to become tenacious and determined, qualities which will ultimately help you to succeed in life. You also learned to think of others first. For years, you always thanked me for staying with you in the hospital and taking you to your doctor appointment, which frankly always amazed me. As if I would have chosen to be anywhere else.

I know how hard you've worked, not only on your bar mitzvah but also on your mitzvah project. Wow, 100 rock walls—as somebody who has never even climbed one wall that is certainly an accomplishment to be proud of! Your motto in life, which seems to be "I'll try my best," really came through for you today. I love how devoted you are to our religion, and I cannot tell you how proud you've made me because the words just don't exist.

Lots of parents use this moment to list their child's many accomplishments, or to plot a course for their child's life. I'm not going to do that, because I don't have any specific ambitions for you. You have so many gifts; you could do anything, really. I want to tell you that it's not so important to set the world on fire, but rather to kindle love in people's hearts and to be a force for what is good in this world.

Jared, I wish you an extraordinary life, one filled with the everyday miracles of love, friendship, children, useful work, and a sense of how precious it all is. You have been a wonderful son and brother, and you will be a great man—a great husband, father and friend. I am so happy to have a front row seat, and I'm so grateful to be your mother.

My Husband's Speech:

Jared, you and I share many passions. And what's great is we have access to all of our passions within easy reach. That's why we have a tennis court in front of our house, a basketball court behind our house, and in the middle, cereal—Lots of cereal. About 30–40 boxes at any one time.

And as you drew life lessons from the slaughtering of goats in your Torah portion, I got to thinking about something else that comes from goats: milk, and of course we all know what milk is good for: cereal! This connection between your Torah portion and cereal did not go unnoticed by me, and inspired me to ponder: how cool would it be to also gain some life lessons from those colorful characters on all those cereal boxes in our cabinet?

So I selected a few of those mascots that personify some of your finest qualities—and I wanted to highlight a few of them now:

Determination…

Best personified by the Trix Rabbit, who never gives up. He shows dogged determination by pursuing Trix cereal, despite continuous set– backs, until the kids bust him by saying "Silly Rabbit, Trix are for kids!" But that doesn't deter him… he is unstoppable, and so are you! And like Rabbit, your determination is what enabled you to come back from your arm injury so you could become a competitive rock climber and tennis player, achieve excellence in your academics and Jewish studies, as evidenced by your outstanding performance today.

Treating others how you'd want to be treated…

Like Cap'n Crunch. He always went the extra mile to rescue kids in danger with his pirate ship and the sweet crunchy taste of Cap'n Crunch. In doing so, he put his ship and crew in great peril. Jared, your manners and the way you put others' needs before your own truly sets YOU apart.

I can't tell you many times we've heard, "Your son has great manners. You really did something right." I wish we could take credit for it, but it's all you. Remember, there's never a rush hour on the road to the extra mile.

Passion

Go coo coo for Cocoa Puffs like Sonny the coo coo bird. Just like Sonny always went coo coo when he finally got his Cocoa Puffs, harness your inner coo coo bird in everything you do. Your passion inspires others to follow… like the passion you showed by climbing 100 rock walls and raising $2200. I saw your passion, and sometimes pain, toward completing the goal. You and Sonny make a great team!

And last but not least, BE GRRREAT!!

Like Tony the Tiger, always keep your positive attitude, while striving for excellence in everything you do.

Jared, it's truly amazing what wonderful traits you have in common with a silly rabbit, a crazy pirate, a coo coo bird, a happy tiger, and even an old goat. Ultimately, it's all about being a good human being, which you already are, and treating people with respect and kindness.

I'm so proud to have you as my cereal buddy, my sports buddy, my son and my friend, I love you.

I Lied, Linda

– Anne Sexton

From Anne Sexton to her 15-year-old daughter Linda, 1969:

Dear Linda,

I am in the middle of a flight to St. Louis to give a reading. I was reading a New Yorker story that made me think of my mother and all alone in the seat I whispered to her "I know, Mother, I know." (Found a pen!) And I thought of you—someday flying somewhere all alone and me dead perhaps and you wishing to speak to me.

And I want to speak back. (Linda, maybe it won't be flying, maybe it will be at your own kitchen table drinking tea some afternoon when you are 40. Anytime.)—I want to say back.

1. I love you.

2. You never let me down.

3. I know. I was there once. I too, was 40 and with a dead mother who I needed still.

This is my message to the 40-year-old Linda. No matter what happens you were always my bobolink, my special Linda Gray. Life is not easy. It is awfully lonely. I know that. Now you too know it—wherever you are, Linda, talking to me. But I've had a good life—I wrote unhappy—but I lived to the hilt. You too, Linda—Live to the HILT! To the top. I love you, 40-year old Linda, and I love what you do, what you find, what you are! —Be your own woman. Belong to those you love. Talk to my poems, and talk to your heart — I'm in both: if you need me. I lied, Linda. I did love my mother and she loved me. She never held me but I miss her, so that I have to deny I ever loved her—or she me! Silly Anne! So there!

XOXOXO
Mom

The Way that Daddy Said Goodbye

– Donna Isaacson

My darling Hanna

Now that you are a little older, I will try to explain why your daddy did not say goodbye to you before he died.

This has been hard for you to understand and hard for me as well.

Your father was the bravest man I have ever known. He tried everything once he was diagnosed with a brain tumor. He commuted to Duke University for an experimental treatment, endured Four surgeries, radiation and chemotherapy. Everything that was offered. He never complained for a minute.

He made a CHOICE. A very singular choice. He refused to admit he was terminally ill. He refused to act like a dying man. He never stayed in the doctor's office after his initial checkup. He would leave before the scans were put up and discussed. He didn't want to know.

He never said goodbye to me either. He always moved in the direction of life. He survived for ten years, eight years longer than expected. The reason I believe is due to the enormous love he had for you and me.

I asked your dad to make a video for you. I wanted him to share things with you that only a father can say to his daughter. "How to behave with boys," "What NOT to do," 'What you should dress like on a first date" silly things like that.

I wanted him to tell you how he made his career choices. To never chase the money but to do what you loved most of all. I wanted him to leave notes behind for your passages into adulthood. So many things I wanted him to talk to you about.

That request was denied, much to my frustration. To do that was to admit that his time was limited. It made me angry and frustrated. I carried that anger too long.

One day I had an epiphany. I realized that this was the last choice he got to make. How he was going to handle the way in which he died. He wanted no "formal" goodbyes, no sad, tearful farewells. He wanted to do it his way. What right did I have to ask him to do it any other way? It would be harder for me, but that was a small price to pay for letting him determine his spiritual path.

So darling, he did say goodbye in his own way.

Many years later, as I was cleaning up, I found an unlabeled video tape. I put it in the VHS and there was your dad telling you how much he loved you. How much he wanted you to choose a career you loved. Many of the things I had asked him to do. He spoke to you for fifteen minutes about family, love, work and how much he loved you. How hard we fought to have you and all the middle of the night feedings he did with you watching old movies at 3 a.m. How you would cuddle up on his chest and both of you fall asleep.

It was beautiful and tender, just as you both were.

Sometimes we just have to walk away and give someone we love a little space to sort things out. He was an amazing man. I haven't met anyone quite like him before or since.

The greatest gift he gave to both of us was "family" and that lives on and on.

Love,
Your Mama

Your First Three Songs

– Corey Becker

Aiden and Logan, my Mini Men:

Saturday, April 26th, 2014

I've thought through this letter a dozen times already. There is so much. I am, unfortunately, not a good enough writer to put in words. Emotionally, sentimentally and hilariously you two have become my everything, in every way children can for their father. As you both probably know by the time you read this, I am an openly sensitive man. I stand by my beliefs, but always consider others. But what I stand by in strength and emotion most is you. I hope I can do my emotions justice in these few pages. I'm writing while listening to the first 3 songs you both heard on your way home from the hospital.

Song 1: Rise Against–Swing Life Away

Aiden. You were the most significant change in my life. Before you, I did not know who I was. Only 25 when you were born, I had already finished my degree, moved across the country twice and married your mother. Arguably I should have known what kind of man I was. But a few years into my television career, I was let go from a very trying job. I came home defeated. Opening the door, my six-month old son squealed in excitement – just to see his Dad. For the next nine months it was you and me. Occasionally working nights, you and I were rarely apart. You had already touched my life by just existing, but as you started having opinions, thoughts and forming words, I found who I was as a man and father. Fatherhood was all I was made for, which you taught me. I rarely remember the boy I was before I was your father. In my hardest times, I had you by my side. Thank you for making me the man I am. A man proud to be your father.

Then came you, Logan. You may read this at a young age or mature one. I hope one day you are able to put yourself in my shoes at the time of your birth. Yes, your mom and I separated before you were one year old. I hope we let you know that this had nothing to do with you. You were planned, a blessing, the happiest thing any of us could imagine. In the hardest time of our lives, you carried us through. You are the glue between your mom, myself and your brother. The greatest blessing we didn't know was coming. You made us complete in our own separate ways. You were Aiden's best friend the minute he held you. You were your mother's greatest achievement (by now you've probably heard a million times how you were almost born on Santa Monica Blvd., making it to the hospital a mere seven minutes before you were born). I see you as the beginning of the happiest time in my life.

Song 2: Anberlin–Fin*

Boys, you must understand that your mom and I had troubles in getting together too young, starting at 16. But without our years together we would never have you. Therefore, it is something neither of us can look back at in regret. In our hardest time though, we got to know the happiest little boy with a smile wider than any of us had seen. Logan, you were what we all needed. You mean more to us than I know how to put into words.

Then came our time that might create some of your first memories... the three of us. We are inseparable. So much so that you both still refuse to sleep in a room I'm not in. In emotional times, pain and loss, difficult path and my greatest successes—you two have been there. Every memory relates to you boys. I have two infinitely loving, happy little boys who I kiss on the forehead and tell I love them every single day. I know no matter what comes my way, you are my reason for living. Every day you save my life... whether you are behaving or not.

I hope in the years that come I can show you my every breath is to make your life better. To raise you, provide for you, and put you in time out when I have to (sorry) is my honor. Feel unconditional love and know that you will forever have your father to turn to. And never turn your back on each other. Because no one else will ever be your brother.

Song 3: Straylight Run–Existentialism on Prom Night

It's hard for a man to try to explain to his sons who he is as a person, especially considering they might read this as men one day. I hope you grow up to understand that people are, in essence, good. They can hurt. They can be hurt past repair. But if you treat others with goodness, you will receive as much as they have in return. I am the luckiest man alive in the love of my friends, my career and the wealth of fatherhood. I received this all by being honest (even when it's hard), giving, and warm to anyone I can reach. It can be difficult sometimes. We all make mistakes. But it is harder and more tiring to be angry than it is to be forgiving. Put yourself in the other person's shoes whenever possible, which is sometimes very hard.

Life is a blessing. You will find time heals all wounds. Learn to weigh value against conflict. The people who matter will always be worth fighting for. Though sometimes a fight lost does not mean it is a fight without value. The best arguments are ones to solve conflict, not to throw gasoline on fires. Do your best to listen instead of wait to talk.

And, above all, respect women. Your Great Grandmother may have been the most important person to touch my life. Your grandmother, aunts, and the many women I call friends are more valuable to me than anyone. Never undervalue or use. Not having sisters, I hope you can learn this. It is very important to me.

Watch Almost Famous, Rocky, and The Shawshank Redemption. Listen to Deftones and Jack's Mannequin. Experience the Friday Night Lights series. Learn the passion of art and that love is worth fighting for. Cry in a movie. Drink a cup of coffee on Santa Monica Beach at 1am, South of the Pier. And never believe being a "man" means you can't be in touch with your emotions. Know your dad loves you, and nothing will ever change that.

With all my heart.
Dad.

All for a Reason Our Souls Have Chosen

– Mary Sheldon

Precious girls,

As far as I'm concerned, all the wisdom in the world is contained within one single bumper sticker: IT'S ALL GOOD.

I believe that we are, every one of us, perfect, inter–connected, and divine sparks of a loving, intelligent Universe, and that we come down to Earth, lifetime after lifetime, for our own amusement and growth. I believe that we make agreements with other souls before we're born, setting the stage for the situations we've chosen to encounter in this incarnation, and that it's all one exhilarating, engrossing game of pretend and illusion, with villains and heroes, trials and triumphs. Nothing happens by chance; everything, no matter how horrible and heartbreaking it may seem, is happening for a reason that our soul has chosen. And when the time comes for us to die, in that moment we'll understand it all, and remember who we really are.

I also believe that we are, above all things, creative – our thoughts, our feelings, and our beliefs have a tremendous impact on our lives – we tend to pull in what we dwell on most often. So it's a good idea to choose wise and loving and positive thoughts!

And, while you're at it, choose wise and loving and positive actions as well. Be madly kind at every opportunity. Shower the people you love with love. Live sensibly, except when you're occasionally being reckless and crazy. Do what makes you happy and fulfilled. Feel free to make "mistakes," if you need to.

But why am I even telling you this? Both of you girls are wiser and kinder than I ever thought about being, and you two have been the greatest teachers I have ever known. Yes, it's all good, as the bumper sticker says, but you girls have transcended that by far: you are better than good – you are the absolute best this universe has to offer.

It's quite the honor, being your mother, and I thank you for choosing me.

Love,
Mama

Chapter 4

Hopes For The Future

Sometimes as a parent I wonder if what I say makes any difference to my kids at all. It's as if there is a small window of opportunity, while children are very young, to say and show everything that will be needed for life. When the teenage years arrive, the window closes. Suddenly they are omniscient. It seems like nothing gets through without force. Judging by my own life, I would say that all the good advice is stored up in there, somewhere, but it's only years later that any of it makes sense, and then, perhaps, it's already too late. Then again, maybe at least some of the good advice sticks. Probably our actions and subconscious habits rub off more than our wise words do. Well, so be it.

It's only natural to want our children to have bright futures. We dream that somehow they will avoid all the mistakes we made, and build on the positives at the same time. Perhaps that's all wishful thinking. Maybe the only reason we're here at all is to be present and available when things don't go according to plan. Sometimes kids need love more than good advice.

Each of us has a slightly different definition of success. Our children might strongly disagree with our own views, and figure out their success on their own terms. It's hard to step back and let things take their course, after what seems like a lifetime of holding their hands and guiding their steps. But step back, and let go we must.

As you read these letters, perhaps you'll find others expressing the very same ideas that were in your own heart. After all, people have far more in common than we like to admit!

Be Leaders to Peace

– Andrew Lientz

Dear Cedar, Pearl, and Atlas,

You will have a lifetime to figure out what you do and how you do it. You will have memories of your Dad that will change as you get older. You will find joy and regret in some way every day. My intention is never to take away your life experiences or make your decisions for you. Watching you make choices has been one of my great joys. When each of you were small, I had this strong hope that you would become an engineer when you got older. As I watched you grow up, I realized how little that mattered. Being your own person and loving your family are the most important things.

There are two lessons I hope you remember from your Dad. The first is simple. Science and math are easy and they are the gateway to a world that most of the world never gets to experience. Even if you have become an artist, learn the language of science and math and find the beauty in numbers and the physics of the world.

The second sounds simple but has taken me a lifetime to understand and try to figure out. In fact, it has been a discussion at work, at home, in volunteer work, everywhere. Be a leader. Leading is the most impactful thing you can do. Sometimes it means being the boss, sometimes it means being a good follower, and sometimes it means questioning authority. You can be a leader of people, a thought leader, or lead by example. In all cases, you make people's lives better and you make a difference.

I could bore you with a thousand stories about my varied career. Instead, I'll give you an example of leading by example... the simplest form of leadership. When we lived in Culver City, I used to jog over to a huge set of stairs at the La Ballona Scenic Overlook. Every time I went up, I looked for trash and put it in my pocket. I'd throw it away at the top. I did it every day. I wasn't showing anyone what to do, I didn't want my park to be dirty and watch the trash go into the ocean so I led the way to a cleaner park. As I bent over to pick something up one day, I heard someone say "That guy just picked up the trash." The next time they stopped and picked up a piece of trash, I knew they had a path to ownership of the shared space from me.

Leadership has various rewards and some days it has none. I have had a number of people tell me "You're the best boss I ever had." I have also had people yell at me when I had to stand in opposition. I wish for you those experiences and everything in between.

We can't always make the right choice or find the right path. Don't expect to. Find leadership in other people. Get them to help you find your path. Those who surround you are the sounding board for you to figure out what to do next. Leadership isn't something that just comes to you. Build your leadership on the people you trust.

Since before you were born, your Mom carried around a framed poster with a quote from Nick Carter. When she first put it up in our apartment in Venice it felt a little preachy to have on display. Ten years later, I rushed to hang it in our new house in Bellevue. This simple quote has come to define the ultimate rule for leaders to me.

If you look around and see a problem, and no one else is doing anything about it—you're elected.

Find a place for it in your house and minds. Carry it with you as a memory of your parents.

When you read this you might remember all the times I asked you to be a leader rather than fighting with each other. You might not. I will remember the looks on your face when I didn't get mad at you, but asked you to find a solution. The frustration that a child feels when they have to lead to peace instead of peace being dictated is a frustration you will feel your entire life. In spite of frustration, leading to peace, a great destination, or the solution to a hard engineering problem have been the hallmarks of my life. As your Dad, I hope my greatest hallmark is leading you to adulthood.

I love you more than the world.
Dad

A Person Whose Heart Is Open

–Jenny Laper

Dear Children,

Have you ever heard the phrase "actions speak louder than words"? Have you noticed how that is often true in your life? Do you think about the ways you can express your best self not so much by what you say, but by what you do?

We tend to think that we cannot make much of a difference in the world just being our everyday selves. Unless we accomplish some great goal, or have an amazing original idea, we are nobody. We forget that each of us can choose at any moment to show kindness to others, to listen and offer understanding to someone who is feeling down, or simply smile at the grocery clerk or the elderly woman sitting alone at the park. Perhaps yours is the first friendly face the clerk or the woman has seen all day, or even all week, and now they feel a little less tired or lonely.

Think of yourself as a person whose heart is open to sharing feelings of love and joy with others each day, whenever you see an opportunity. Your little brother or sister, or new friend, may need you to show them how to kick the soccer ball, or jump from the diving board, or pronounce a new word. When you offer help cheerfully, and because you want others to succeed and feel good, you are contributing something very important to the world, and to yourself. You are helping to create harmony and happy feelings, instead of sadness or anger or loneliness, and you will find that your kindness towards others helps you to feel stronger and happier also.

Do you sometimes forget that you have a long list of people and things in your life to be grateful for? We all have those days when we imagine that everyone else is better off, has more "stuff" or a bigger bedroom or a nicer parent. When those days happen, if you can start remembering all the stuff you so love in your life, all the times your mom or dad or best friend or quirky Auntie made you laugh, or surprised you with an unexpected gift or treat, you will probably start feeling Gratitude. It is hard to feel bad when you are feeling thankful, especially when you say "thank you" either with words, or by thinking of some small thing you might do for someone else, rather than sitting there feeling sorry for yourself.

Start noticing all the opportunities you have every day to open your heart and take action. No action is too small to make a difference. Maybe someone drops a pen and you pick it up for her, or you tell your friend who wiped out on his skateboard a funny story, or write a silly poem for your Mom when she is having a hard day. By choosing kindness in those moments, you are spreading joy and love where it is needed. That is an important accomplishment!

Live Your Adventure

– Rachel Gruman Bender

Dear Allie and Zoe,

Hi, my loves. We are going to have many conversations over the years. I want to keep an open dialog with you both, and I hope that you can always come to me whenever you're sad, confused, hurt, or in trouble, as well as during happy times, too. I will try my best to listen and to be patient and respectful of you and hope you'll do the same.

And while we'll have many conversations about many things over my lifetime, there are a few important pieces of advice I've learned over the years that I'd like to share with you both. I hope it's helpful:

Know your worth. It's natural to seek approval from others. But it's more important to look inwards and know in your heart of hearts that you are worthy and valuable. If someone—a boyfriend or a friend—doesn't treat you with kindness and respect, say something to them. If their behavior doesn't change, let this person go. I realize that may not be easy, but knowing that you deserve much better will give you the strength to let go. Relationships should only add good things to your life—they should build you up, not tear you down or make you feel bad or less than. Try not to get so caught up in making someone else happy that you neglect your own happiness.

Love your body. It's the only one you'll ever have. Some days you won't be happy with certain parts, but all of the parts are beautiful. You can run, jump, dance, swim, do headstands, and hug, thanks to your body. It's an amazing tool. Be mindful of and kind with the words you choose to describe your body, even if it's just to yourself. Stay away from people, websites, and magazines that make you feel bad about your body. Focus instead on moving your body until you break a sweat and fueling it with good nutrition, which will keep you happy and healthy and help you live a long life—all of the things your dad and I so want for you both.

Check in with yourself. Set aside some time for reflection, even if it's just 10 minutes a few times a week. It's good to check in with your body, your heart, and your mind. Is there anything you would like to work on or improve? Is your job/relationship heading in a direction you feel happy with? Does it/he/she make you happy? If not, it's time to reassess and think about what steps will get you closer to your goal—to your dreams—and start heading in that direction instead. Think of yourself as a sailboat tacking in the wind, making adjustments as you go to ensure that you're heading in the right direction, whatever that means to you.

Practice gratefulness. I think it's one of the keys to being a happy person, and there is so much to be thankful for in our lives. One easy way to practice gratefulness on a daily basis is to pay attention to the small things: how good it feels to have a warm breeze sweep through your hair; the feeling of sunshine warming your back (while slathered in SPF 30); getting a series of green traffic lights when you're in a hurry; or just laughing with your sister. Find your own versions of these little treasures throughout your day—just notice them and take them in. They will multiply your happiness.

See the world. Having a formal education is important, and so is seeing the world. Exploring different countries and cultures is a key part of your education. When I was growing up, your Great Grandma Selma took me, along with Marmie, to many different places across the globe— your Great Grandma lived for adventure and had been to nearly every country in the world. We rode camels and climbed inside the pyramids in Egypt, ate borscht in Russia, sailed on a yacht in Turkey, and much more. It was amazing and opened up my eyes to the beautiful variety of cultures and lifestyles in the world. It showed me that there is no one right way to live (as long as you are not hurting anyone else, of course)—just many options. Your dad and I plan to take you both all over the world for as long as we're able to. No matter what, keep exploring. Use your passport. It's a true ticket for adventure.

Live your life. I had been trying to get pregnant for a while when your dad and I decided to check a trip off of his wish list—Antarctica—whether or not our last attempt at getting pregnant was successful. Naturally, we found out I was pregnant a few weeks before our trip (we didn't know it was twins at this point). That didn't stop us from going on an adventure. We flew to the very tip of South America—called El Fin del Mundo, aka "The End of the World"—and hopped on board a ship set to sail around Antarctica. We made it through 40– foot waves hammering our ship, climbed snow– covered mountains, sat in a small rubber boats as humpback whales breached the icy waters, all while my ski pants got progressively tighter.

The point is: Don't put your life on hold just because you're waiting for something big to happen. Keep living your life and things will fall into place the way they're supposed to—or maybe they won't, but that's okay, too.

When your dad and I came back from Antarctica, I had my first ultrasound. When my doctor told us I was pregnant with twins, we burst into tears of joy. About four hours later, we panicked. Twins? When we calmed down, we realized how doubly blessed we were to have you both at the same time, entering our lives together so we wouldn't miss a single minute with either of you. We wouldn't have it any other way.

Above all, know that you both are deeply and incredibly loved by your dad and I—more than we could ever express in words. We love you to pieces and always will. Now, get out there and enjoy all that the world has to offer. We'll be right here, any time you need us.

Love,
Mom

Mame's Philosophy

– Nancy Gersh

Dear Bennett,

Being your mom, or as you say, some "Mame" version thereof, has been the greatest privilege of my life. You are such an intelligent, handsome, creative, compassionate and funny guy. You have such a unique way of viewing the world. You're a complete original. Thank you for still loving The Nutcracker and going along with my love of Priscilla Queen of the Desert and all the other colorful and sparkly things of the world. Thank you for your love of animals and for the support you've always given to me.

I know I can't compete with your favorite "Modern Family" episode, "Phil's Philosophy," but here's my humble version.

Make your life your own masterpiece. Don't settle.

Order a la Carte. Choose only what you love. Quality over quantity. "Feasible" is the F word. Dream big and figure out how to live your dreams. Don't suffer fools. Too many do. That's why there are so many fools and so much needless suffering.

Never forget a kindness. Repay it with gratitude and then pay it forward.

Live the quote, "You have not lived today until you have done something for someone who can never repay you."

Leave the world a little better than you found it.

Fight for what you believe is right. Truth matters. Speak for those who can't speak.

Make each day an adventure. Find beauty and fun in the smallest things of everyday life.

Live a life rich in magic moments...the perfect sunset, rooftop view, falling in love, saving a life.

You are the greatest joy in my life. As you always used to say to me, "I love you till the end of the counting."

Mom

My Mantras on Living
– Glynis Gerber

Dear Beloved Children and Grandchildren: I recently experienced a very unsettling take off from Houston International. It was during those few minutes when we were all uncertain of whether the plane could actually take off safely that my mind turned to my children and grandchildren. Had I said the proper goodbyes, were our relationship solid and had I made a positive difference in the lives they lead as adults? And then the panic subsidized and I realized that I have had a wonderful life and if the plane were to crash, I would have few regrets. But it was with that fragility in mind that I want to convey a message to you, my children and grandchildren–the light of my life.

These are a few truisms that I think are my life's mantras–I wear them like clothing. I hope in this short letter I impart some of that wisdom to you all.

1. Don't do anything that would embarrass your children or parents. Live a life that is honest.

2. Your attitude determines your altitude; Not always easy to live by, especially if things like health are an issue. But being the happiest 'you' or the most positive 'you' is important. By exuding a feeling of happiness and stability, people around you will benefit from your attitude. When something gets your down, or you feel like you can't cope, have a positive mechanism to turn your mood around—a hot shower, a long walk, watch a sitcom for 1/2 an hour. Find something simple that makes you feel good, and turn your mood around, without turning to destructive habits.

3. You don't always have to be right. It's okay to disagree. This is a lesson that I have found hard to live by. But if you have to be right in the relationship, then the other person has to be wrong – and that puts a tremendous strain on any relationship.

4. You don't have to offer advice or fix things. Sometimes, just listening is enough. Sometimes, the other person has to fix their issues.

5. You can only be responsible for your own life, once your children become adults. Yes, I would like them to do things 'my way', and yes, I would like them to think like me, and do good deeds and try to have stable relationships, but I can't control their lives. They have to

self-generate the life they want.

6. Leave a foot print. By giving to family, friends and your community, both Jewish and secular, you leave a footprint and make a difference. However small, every time I do something positive for someone else it makes someone's life easier, or my community better.

7. My love for my family has no boundaries; if I am fortunate to be on the giving side of the relationship, I try to give with a full heart. It's a fortunate place to be.

8. Know your place; Respect the relationship between husbands and wives and their family.

9. Cherish the uniqueness of each child and each grandchild. It doesn't matter that they are all different, as long as they are good people with good values, they have accomplished a lot. Tell them that you love them often. Hug them too.

10. Honor 'good citizenship' and honest values. The world is too small, don't compromise your values. It's a slippery slope, once you compromise for this, then you compromise for that, and so forth.

11. Have fun and do creative things. It's nice to vary your life. It doesn't have to be expensive, just creative.

12. Make every Shabbat fun and all the Jewish holidays special and fun, so much so, that other families want to be with you and want you at their table. I have made it a priority to make the holidays fun with games, table set ups and interesting menus, and guests. And also I have tried to make Shabbat different from any other day of the week. The food is fresher, the table looks good, I use china, and separate this day from the other six.

13. My Mother– in– law, Doreen, of blessed Memory, always said that only in the dictionary does 'success' come before 'work'. Have a solid work ethic – and always pitch in to help.

My blessing to you all is "May my children's children be blessed to lead full rich Jewish lives and may they live to see grandchildren thrive in peace."

Love Safti

Passion & Purpose
– Jill O'Neal

To my beloved sons, Owen Ray and Lucas Holt O'Neal:

I title this letter "A Lesson in Life: Living a Happy, Meaningful Life with Purpose."

I'm going to start off by sharing with you one of my life experiences that, to this day, has provided a lifelong lesson that has dramatically impacted my journey of life. It's about a single decision I made when I was just 18 years old.

Your grandfather always wanted the best for my future. He wanted my future to be brighter than his past. He didn't have a college education and ended up working multiple 16-hour shifts at the railroad, with hardly a day to spend with our family. And this is why he was so adamant about me going to college. I was adamant that I was going to college too! But, he wanted me to have a career "where the jobs were." He wanted me to be an engineer. I wanted to create jobs. I wanted to own a dance studio. But I didn't want to disappoint him, so I followed his plan. After three long years of struggling through engineering classes, I decided it was time to compromise. I also didn't want to start all over, so I did the best I could with the credits I had: a degree in math and business, which has served me well. For the last nearly 14 years I have had a career that pays well. I have a skill set that's in demand. I've never had to worry about finding a job. But from one position to the next and from one company to the next, two very important components were always missing. Passion and purpose.

I truly believe my dad wanted the very best for me and gave me the best advice he knew how to provide. I only wish I had been stronger to follow my heart. To follow my passion. To make a decision to do something that I was passionate about, that I loved. I discovered that when I did anything without passion and without purpose, it became meaningless and I never found true happiness. I was always looking to fill the void with something else.

Promise me you will always follow your heart, even if other's frown. You have only one precious life on this earth. Your life is your journey – not mine, not your father's, not anyone else's – it's yours! Know that you are loved beyond what I can write in words and that your life has meaning and purpose. You give it meaning. You give it purpose. You are in charge of creating a life of happiness. And so I leave you with this:

Mom's 20 Daily Mental Vitamins for a Happy, Meaningful, Purposeful Life:

1. Fear God in every decision and choice you make.
2. Start and end each day with a positive heart.
3. Take chances and try new things. You'll discover something new about yourself.
4. Be led by passion, not wealth.
5. Make mistakes. Learn and grow from your mistakes.
6. Talk to God.
7. Don't be afraid of change.
8. My dad always said, "Haste makes waste." Take your time and do things right the first time.
9. Smile. Laugh.
10. Be Confident.
11. Pay someone a compliment.
12. Be Genuine.
13. Lend a hand to someone in need.
14. Find something you love…and do it well…
15. …and passionately…
16. …and you will be able to make a living of it.
17. Follow your heart.

I love you most,
Mom

Be a Possibillion

– Jeff McMahon

Dear Brayden and Mackena,

Everyone has life advice to share, and most people will share it freely and unsolicited. So, why shouldn't I? Seek advice, take advice, be a good listener, and decide for yourself if and how you'll use others' advice. You can't benefit from the words of wisdom you decline to take and you can't be hurt by the foolish advice you never use. Seek happiness for yourself and help others find happiness, too.

What does it mean to be happy? To answer that question you need to know yourself and be honest with yourself. Maybe family makes you happy, maybe friends, maybe your job, maybe money, maybe all or none of those things. When you discover what makes you happy, embrace it, but be open to the possibility that what makes you happy can change.

I wish nothing more than for each of you to have opportunities throughout your life to pursue what makes you happy and to enjoy being happy. But, do not expect life to go a certain way. If you have expectations for things in life, you are bound to have disappointment and unhappiness. If you have acceptance for things in life, you will be less disappointed and more open to happiness you might not even have expected. I am not telling you to have low expectations or low standards. Have high expectations and high standards, and demand excellence of yourself and others, but also practice the art of accepting the things you can do nothing to change. Life happens quickly, and even when we know what we want out of life, many forces often prevent us from getting it, and we end up disappointed. If you just accept life for what it is, you will have many opportunities for happiness and that is something you can expect!

Assuming you've got the happiness thing down for yourselves, how do you help others to find happiness? Respect and kindness will go quite far in helping others find happiness. If you have respect for others, you value their individuality and you understand their wants and needs may not be the same as yours, but they are equally as valid and important. If you are kind to others, the effect on happiness for them and everyone they are kind to will be massive. Whenever possible, you can give of your time and/ or money to impact others' happiness, but do so because you want to, not because you feel it is expected.

Alright, here are some things I've learned about life:

No one knows what they are doing or if they are doing it right. This goes for adults, the president, teachers, bosses, me, you, and everyone to come.

Accepting that there is no such thing as a "grown- up" makes it a lot easier to enjoy life like a kid.

Kids are amazing. They live life happily and know how to have fun. Observe them and learn.

Many teenagers suck. They do not know how to live life happily and they are not respectful or kind.

The least respectful and kind teens you will meet growing up have no idea why they are being hurtful. Accept that they exist, but don't let them impede your pursuit of happiness.

The teenage years will be awkward and painful, but they don't last forever. Believe in yourself and don't worry about "fitting in" too much. What it means to fit in will be something altogether different once high school is over, and different again once you're out of your twenties.

Enjoy the outdoors, the sun, nature, and being active.

Enjoy books, movies, video games, and just sitting on the couch indoors. Try sports. Challenge yourself and just try to do your best.

Learn about animals. Specifically dogs. Forming a bond with a dog is simple and wonderful in ways that bonding with a human will never be.

Indulge in sweets now and then, get into a heated debate with relatives at a holiday gathering, or go fishing every day of the summer.

Cut back on those sweets, leave the hot button topics out of family gatherings, skip a day of fishing and get a boring house project done.

Respect science and learning. People who spend their lives seeking out answers to the "hows and whys" of life usually find out some pretty useful and cool information.

Be a possabillion. That means staying open to many ideas about the universe and everything in it unless overwhelming factual evidence exists to dispel an idea or eradicate a fact. Over and over in the history of mankind we have been really wrong about some key facts, but we seem to get better with time, so there shouldn't be any "the world's not flat" kind of revelations unless we get dumber as a society.

Mankind is harming the planet. Releasing carbon dioxide into the atmosphere and polluting the oceans with trash. There's not much we can do about it, but we should at least own up to it.

If you're looking for love, look for someone you can be best friends with. Don't be afraid of dying. You won't know what it's like to be gone. Don't be afraid of living and trying things that are new, different, not your typical choice, because one day you will die and it will have been more important to have had some kind of experience rather than none at all.

Laugh a lot. Make jokes, but be careful not to make them at the expense of others, or at least cancel that out by making lots at your own expense.

Don't ever take life so seriously that you feel like quitting at it. It's a miracle we exist at all, and a shame not to enjoy every bit of life we have.

Seriously, have some fun and be happy. Nothing matters if you're not happy.

Be wise with money, but don't be too foolish about storing it up. You never know when tragedy could strike and end it all, so enjoy what you have now and sock a little bit away just in case you go on into your nineties.

Learn a little bit about everything you can. Just enough to know when a professional is being deceitful with you (mainly mechanics, handymen, and insurance agents), but not so much that all of your friends and relatives are always hitting you up to help with projects and solve their problems.

Know that you will always have people in your life who know just how amazing you are. If you need to know this at any time, seek out mom and dad.

If you need help, don't be afraid to ask.

Just by existing, you make many people happy. That wasn't so hard, was it? Have a great time living life. Really do. And, if you figure out any secrets to doing it right, let me be the first to know.

I love you to pieces, kids.
Dad

Boys and Girls: Be Confident

– DJ Melzer

Dear Huntley and Jack,

We love you both more than anything in this world and you taught us a love we didn't know until we met the two of you. Momma and Dadda have a few words for you.

Love each other and love others. Family is everything, so take care of them, love them and respect them. Love yourselves the way we love you and never tolerate disrespect, especially from yourself. Be kind to others even those who don't deserve it because it's a reflection of you. Surround yourselves with others who are kind and happy because life is too short for anything else. Life will be full of choices and if you don't like the results, make new choices because it's never too late. Home is not where we live, it's who we are and you will always be loved and welcome at home.

Jack: Be confident. Be kind to girls, and NEVER break up with a girl over the phone. Shower everyday with soap and cut your nails. Always put the toilet seat down. Learn how to do your laundry and always eat breakfast.

Huntley: Be confident. Never lose yourself and be true to your dreams. Don't chase something that is running (i.e. men). Learn to stay organized and NEVER gossip. Take care of your hair and skin and love yourself. Learn how to drive a stick shift and don't be afraid to get dirty.

Lastly, patience, kindness, trust, love, self– respect, respect for life, faithfulness, forgiveness and peace never steered anyone wrong. Remember these words and live by them in life as you live your lives to the fullest. You deserve that!

Loving you every moment of every day,
Mommy and Dad

Things That Have Been Left Unsaid

– Vic Edwards

Dear Steph and Sam,

I take to my heart to write you this letter today. You are both growing up very fast and sometimes it seems as if the weeks and years are passing faster for me. With that, there are many things that I have already said to you and a vast amount if things that have been left unsaid.

Love conquers all. Emotions and timing are not always in sync for adults as well as me. I find myself shouting at either one or both of you when I should be showing patience and wisdom. I also find myself very loving and giving into to you when I should have been more stern and steadfast. Overall, I love you both and I will always remind the both of you that no matter what is said or what you do, I will still always love you. Please strive to be a more patient parent than I have been and learn from my mistakes.

Love your work. In your profession and work you choose, you must do what you love. It may always seem like you have plenty of time on this planet to come and go as you please. The truth is that your life spans are finite, so the time you spend should be spent well. This is the reason you must enjoy whatever you do in life for time is not in your favor. There is no free lunch in this world, unless you are a forest animal. But even the forest animals pay of a price in the end, especially if they become someone else's lunch.

Enjoy learning. I hope you both always have a life of learning. The written word is a treasure. It can make you explore all of your emotions or it can take you away to a distant land. I am very proud that you both show a love for reading. You should read many books to your children as I did to you when you were younger. You both use to beg for me to read you a bedtime story. Sometimes those stories came out of my head and of course you felt like dad was "pulling your leg." Just as they say that the open hand receives more than the closed fist, the same is true for your brain or mind.

Fall down a lot. I know that I do not say this often, but it is okay for you to make mistakes. Just make sure that you learn from them and do not repeat them. You both must remember that you are in charge of your lives and you will determine where life takes you in the future by your actions in the present and past. Think about scientists for a moment. Have you ever heard a scientist say "hey, I am going make a whole bunch of mistakes until I find the right answer"? You don't because that is what scientists call conducting experiments.

Money is a tool. As you grow up and get older, you will see both value and virtue in money. You have been taught the three key uses for money: spending, saving and charity. You both should never try to live beyond what you can afford for yourself and your families. If you follow this rule, you will not waste time searching for what you don't have in life. Instead, spend that time with your families. My first statement is important in the fact that one day you too will leave this planet and all the money and possessions you have at that time will become worthless to you.

Find your refuge. There are many times in your life that you will feel worn out or exhausted. You should always have some "me time." Whether that is reading a book on the couch or fishing on a boat, you will need to spend some time by yourself. Use some of this time to reflect on your day, week, or life in general. If you forget how to do it, take a breezy day then stand in the sunshine and let the wind float through your hair.

Make good friends. It is important that you both find good close friends who share commonalities with you. Your friends should be people you can trust. If you look at your friends, who among them would you give your first born child to raise and take care of? Use this definition to determine who your true friends are.

Choose a good mate. Finding the right partner to share your life with can be a difficult task. Although, they should meet the test to be "good friend," they will be more than this. One of the key ways to tell if they are "the one" is if you feel like a part of you is missing when they are not around. You will also need to remember that whether you are living with someone or married, it does require a certain amount of work. Sometime that work requires compromise on your part. It is okay to stand up against your partner, but if it means you will be left standing alone, then you need to remember what is most important for the both of you.

The early moments we shared. When you both were first born, I was thinking, "Oh my God, how am I going to take care of this little thing." At the moment, my heart fell to my feet. It happened with both of you. Everything seemed monumental to me every time you hit a milestone. From the time you first crawled to the time you first walked to the time you started talking. In fact, I felt that my heart was perpetually going to my feet. But no matter what happened, my heart would quickly return to its rightful place once I saw that beautiful smile on both of your faces. Those are the moments I will never forget and the ones you may eventually share with your sons and daughters.

Love,
You Dad

See Beauty. Appreciate Beauty. Create Beauty.

– Linda Fenster

Just as you can see thousands of flowers in a field, all in different colors and shades, so is the world full of all different people who have different beliefs, different languages and ways. Be tolerant and accepting.

Try to be happy and have a positive outlook on life. If you feel sad, then that is okay too. But when you start thinking about sad things all the time try to think of something else like a walk on the beach full of shells and seagulls or a movie you liked. We are in charge of our thoughts just like when you are driving a car. You can drive down a road littered with trash or you can take the scenic route, so it is with your mind, you can steer it in the right direction.

Try to be forgiving when people annoy you. Usually the thing that annoys you in a person is something that you may even do yourself. Be tolerant. When someone is grumpy or mean there is usually a reason they are that way. It may mean they had a mean mom or dad or lost someone they loved. You never know. Sometimes if you smile at someone who is mean or say something nice to them they will feel better.

Be kind to people and be kind to animals. Animals are not here for us to hurt. Animals have special powers. Some dogs and dolphins can tell when a human is sick and they nudge the person in a certain way to let them know. Some dogs help people and guide them when they cannot see. Do you know that elephants are very smart and sensitive too and when one of their elephant family or friends dies, they mourn just like people do when their loved ones die. Some elephants can learn to paint pictures and play soccer.

Think about what you eat. It is important to eat fruits and vegetables every day and also chicken or fish. It helps your whole body be strong and work properly. It is fun to eat cake and candy sometimes too.

Do not take drugs unless the doctor gives you pills when you are sick. Drugs can mess you up very badly and even kill you.

Try not to buy what you do not need. Instead share what you already have if you have a lot of stuff. Lighten your load.

If you are able to help others please do. If you see a hungry person and are able to buy them a sandwich and a drink, do so. Sometimes people fall on hard times and cannot help it that they live on the street help them if you can by sending donations. People who live on the street don't want to, it happened through circumstances. There are schools in poor areas, it would be nice to sometimes send them school supplies and some fun things like stickers or magic markers to make the kids happy.

If you ever think that you are 'hot stuff' for more than a week, go down to the vast ocean and stand there quietly and realize that you are actually quite small.

Be true to yourself. See beauty Appreciate beauty Create beauty

It will fill you up—much more than shopping for things you don't need. Write a story and draw pictures to go with it, hike in the mountains, swim in the sea, tell stories, play sports, be happy and healthy and wish this for all other living beings too.

Love,
Linda

Torchbearers on a Grand Mission

– Jeffrey and Jennifer Schuller

Dearest Dina, Ben, Gavi, Elianna, Zekey, Cobi, and Annalea,

As six of the seven of you are at camp, some local, one in Canada, and another in Israel, we have a brief moment to catch our breath and reflect on life. What makes life worth living? If we have properly done our job, and been half– decent role models, we hope that at least one of your immediate answers would be, "To make the world a better place!"

What that means to you, and what that will come to mean over time, is unique for each person. It is pleasant, and sometimes even euphoric, if others share your meaning. It can be even more blissful when it is shared, nurtured and promoted with your spouse and certainly your children. G-d has blessed us that, as a couple, and now as a family, we have been able to transmit our humble understanding of how to make the world better.

We have been blessed into a faith that did not compel us to recreate the wheel in order to figure it out. As Jews, we have a rich history, tradition and faith dating back over 3300 years ago with the giving of the Ten Commandments on how to live. As you have learned, and will continue to learn, those "simple" ten laws are a mere fraction of what you can embrace in order to reveal G-d in this world.

The beauty of Judaism is that we are taught each person is special and contains a spark of G-d within. Your soul is holy and your time here matters. Your physical presence, the acts you do, and even some you refrain from doing, each miraculously contributes to the betterment of the world.

The great Chasidic forefather, The Baal Shem Tov, said that a leaf does not fall without it being directed by G-d. The world is constantly being created and re-created, and for really one main point. G-d wants to be manifest in our physical world. And he needed you, and each one of us, to help him partner in that utopian vision where only goodness will shine.

So the way we have channeled our mission is in creating what we believe are the finest torchbearers to continue making the world a better place. Each of you is good—so wonderfully good that it brings tears to our eyes. Each of you is gifted and talented in a distinct way. Where one is gregarious and an extrovert, another is a bit shy and private. Where one excels at Math, another is an artist. Where one is sensitive, another is bold. Where one is an old soul, another is a joker. And the list goes on. But, in each of your G-d given strengths, and if you can believe it, even in your challenges, you are on a grand mission. You are here for a reason– and likely more than one. Being privileged and blessed to be your parents, we now know our reason, or should we say seven reasons.

We love you and bless you. May you be a vessel for good, an agent for inspiration and the motivator for helping those around you. May your time on earth not only bring you the awesome awareness of love, purpose and spirituality, but also cause you to deliver it to others.

We thank G-d and you for the gift of being your parents.

Love,
Mommy and daddy

Chapter 5

Old Fashioned Values
For A New World

Things have certainly changed since Grandad's days. The world has become more open in many ways. Race, gender and religious issues have been thrashed out, at least to some degree in our country. We're learning to get along better as a global family too, though many of the same old problems haven't changed. It's certainly not a perfect world.

On the positive side, though, something like love will never get old.

We can be sure that in another fifty or one hundred years, parents will still care about their children, and children will still need acceptance, guidance and love.

Advances in medicine have made it possible to have entirely new kinds of families. But besides the biological technicalities, we find that these families are not that different, after all. The same rules apply. Some kids are adopted, and many others have double families

— one with their biological mother, and another with their biological father. It's a brave new world, but fortunately there is still a place for old fashioned values—the kind that never have an expiration date.

Most of the letters in this collection are the traditional, regular variety. But some are clearly not. Fortunately, love makes room for all of us.

No Dreadlocks, Please

– Dax Shelby

Dear Z

Hate is a strong word. There is a clear distinction between "strongly dislike" and "hate" and I've done my best to use this H-word carefully in my life, reserving it for things that I absolutely abhor and not just those that I casually despise. For example, I hate tomatoes. I strongly dislike green peppers. I hate anti–Semites. I strongly dislike anti–Americans. I hate when the Yankees lose. I strongly dislike when the Red Sox win. You get it. Pretty standard stuff.

And so, it is with clear understanding that I tell you that while I love nearly every classification and genre of music, I hate reggae. Hate it. I find the music lazy, the lyrics uninspiring. Don't get me wrong, I've tried to like it. Back in college, when every other person owned Bob Marley's "Legend" album, I gave it my best shot. Still, I came up empty. My friends would tell me that I just didn't "get" it, that I needed to be stoned to truly appreciate reggae. To that I said, any music that comes with the disclaimer that you have be high to really get, is inherently shitty music.

For the most part, though, reggae is usually hidden safely away in dorm rooms, Jamaican resorts, and marijuana dispensaries. That is with the exception of 1988 when Bobby McFerrin's "Don't Worry, Be Happy" was unleashed upon the masses. To say that this was a national sensation would be an understatement. It was inescapable. It was played at ballparks across America, sung at Elementary School assemblies. Even the Senior Citizens in assisted– living complexes were encouraged to wheeze out the words through their respirators. The song was everywhere. Think "Macarena" or "Gangnam Style" only so much worse. At least those had a fun dance to go along with them. This, however, was a perfect storm of everything I dislike in music: a novelty chorus combined with the aforementioned reggae beat. And, somehow, no one needed to get stoned to enjoy it.

However, as much as I disliked the acapella tune, what I truly hated was the message. Don't worry, be happy. Even my then still, unformed thirteen– year old brain knew there was something wrong with this philosophy.

Don't worry, be happy. Don't worry about the mounting threats of foreign and domestic terrorists. Be happy. Don't worry about chemically treated food products, an alarming national obesity issue, a surge in autism diagnoses in children. Be happy. Don't worry about the shrinking middle class, skyrocketing debt, gender inequality. Be happy.

Still, 26 years later, the more mature and experienced me can concede that Mr. McFerrin may have actually gotten some of it correct. The truth is, buddy, there will be plenty of things in your life to have anxiety over that you need to recognize those things that you shouldn't worry about.

For example, don't worry about getting straight A's. Leave that to the nerds and the kids with the fancy tutors. All I want is for you to try your best, understand what you're being taught instead of just memorizing facts, and to learn how to think for yourself. When you're an adult, no one cares about the grades you got when you were younger. So be happy, and find that perfect balance between studying and having fun.

Don't worry about keeping up with the Joneses. I don't know who these Joneses are but, most likely, they got a lot of their money from their parents. They're also probably miserable since they've never known what it means to struggle and, thus, can't appreciate the things that have always been provided for them. They'll undoubtedly wind up divorced, in therapy, hooked on pills, and then found dead in a tragic murder/ suicide that will be front page news for a good month. Sordid details will emerge afterwards about the kinds of freaky things these people were mixed up with. These rumors will haunt their children and their children's children for years to come. So yeah, don't worry about keeping up with the Joneses. Be happy that you're not the Joneses.

Don't worry about death. It's going to happen. To you, me, and everyone we both know and love. Really shitty to think about, I know. So try not to. We're all going to die someday, so be happy and embrace the time that you're here instead of freaking out about the time when you won't be.

Don't worry about the window you'll inevitably shatter, the toy you'll break, the fender you'll dent. Yeah, I'll be pissed in the moment, but that moment will pass. And the truth is, that stuff is just glass, plastic, and metal. And it's all replaceable. Be happy that you didn't cut yourself on the broken glass or injure yourself in the fender bender. But don't think for a second that I'm paying for any of that shit.

Finally, and most importantly, don't worry about what other people think. All too often, we allow ourselves to be crippled by the fear of "what others will say," preventing us from doing what we truly desire. You know what I've learned in almost forty years? Other people don't matter. I can't express this enough. Other people don't matter. The only person's opinion that should truly matter to you is your own. Are you proud of the things you say, proud of the things you do? If you can look in the mirror and know that a good, happy person is staring back, this is all that matters.

We live in a sometimes scary, unpredictable world and there's no telling what the next year, day, or even minute, holds in store for us. It would be irresponsible and impractical to tell you not to worry about anything. Just try not to worry about everything. And, when possible, be happy. Because really, what do you have to be unhappy about? You're healthy, free, and have a lifetime of possibility still ahead of you.

And best of all, you have a father who will always love you. No matter what. Even if you come home one day, eating a tomato, denouncing Judaism, and wearing a Red Sox hat. I'll still love you, son.

Just don't even think about showing up in dreadlocks, playing an island beat on a set of bongos, or I'll f#%king disown you.

Love,

Dad

We Will Continue To Share

– Dana Laurence

Dear Isabel,

I do not know when you will read this. I do not know where. I do not know if you will call me after. Or sit down with me. Maybe you will hold my hand. Or just remember who I am and what we shared.

It doesn't matter. We will have shared already, and we will continue to share.

Diapers and bottles. "Ouchies" and tears.

Nana's and the "lello" house. Telephones. Text messages. Bicycles. And Chairs.

Towels at the beach and after a bath. Blankets on grassy fields and beaches.

Your life. My life. Mommy's life. Our lives. Moments. Memories. You know me now, as I write this. I am "daddy." You will know me when you read this. I may still be "daddy." Or "dad." Maybe sometimes even "damn it dad."

I have known you since before you were born, and I will know you when I die. You will hold my hand then, and whisper in my ear. No matter where you are, near or far. And I will love you.

Forever.

Daddy Dana

Extraordinary Possibleatarians

– Lisa Korbatov

As a parent we are convinced that our children are special in just about every way.

Children are the embodiment of hope, unconditional love and our aspirations. I have told my children that "extraordinary people are actually ordinary people who do extraordinary things." It is an observation through the lens of time and some wisdom, and yes, I think it is demonstrated in history and in our own lives.

Ordinary people believe only in the possible. People who strive to be extraordinary actually will not visualize the mere possible or maybe the probable but rather the impossible. By visualizing the impossible, magically they begin to see the possible. Extraordinary acts rely on those with the ability to mix tenacity with optimism. They are irrepressible and their energy is contagious. Think of these people as possibleatarians, anything is possible for them. A French writer, sums it up for me…

"Man cannot discover new oceans unless he has the courage to lose sight of the shore."

So let's be clear: The extraordinary is not the birthright of a privileged or chosen few, but of all people, even the most quiet and humblest among us. There are running threads that exist in these people, a narrative that I think is the undercurrent of their theme of life.

I think that these people would tell you that one of the most effective ways for transcending the ordinary and moving into the realm of extraordinary is saying "yes" more frequently and eliminating "no" almost completely. Of course saying "yes," is in reference to all things that are lawful and not harmful!

The most successful people ignore the odds, they are not stymied by naysayers or those realistic types who live their fears and admonitions, not their hopes and aspirations. The greatest ideas and most extraordinary people might have known the odds of failing and the small percentage of succeeding but took the chance anyway.

If you say you "can" or you say your "can't" both will invariably become true.

Each of our children are unique and I truly believe that no child is ordinary. You are all different and special and one of a kind, down to your DNA.

Ask yourself these questions:

How will you use your gifts? What choices will you make? Will inertia be your guide or will you follow a passion? Will you be original? Will you seek a life of ease or one of adventure and service? Will you wilt under pressure or criticism or follow your heart and your convictions? Will you play it safe or be a bit of a swashbuckler?

When it's tough will you give up or be relentless and persevere? Will you be a builder or a cynic? And all along the way on this journey – can you be kind?

What you choose to do with life and how you arrive at these answers is the secret that will begin to unfold as your journey unfolds.

But before you know it, childhood will draw to a close and you will be getting ready for adulthood and life choices.

Your work is your signature, so autograph it always in excellence. So as you author this life—your life—most people would assume that success and excellence is the result of discipline and determination. It is. But it all really starts with a great attitude. So fill your mind with great thoughts. You will never go any higher that what you think.

Of course there will be obstacles, optimistically referred to as "teachable moments." Sometimes you sail with the wind and sometimes against it; but it is always up to you to adjust your sails. Extraordinary people see the future because they can create it with their energy, courage, hard work and passion.

Oh, and as you realize your potential in the years to come, once again, remember that the extraordinary among us can also be nice. In the end we are our choices. Choose wisely and boldly and you will live an extraordinary life.

In closing, I want to tell you that most people don't dwell on these fundamental truths. Extraordinary people are ordinary people who put their heart and soul into whatever they set out to do. So wherever you go, go with all your heart and it will make all the difference.

Love.

Mom

My Perfectly Average Wonder

– Catherine Lacey Dodd

Dearest Callum,

You know how much you were wanted, right? I mean every day I dreamt of having you. I hold you in such great esteem because you are that great backbone that brings it all together, a man in a little boy's skin. A mischievous little look when you know, a look of cheekiness, and getting something more than you could ever have expected.

We had five days together, pretty much entirely by ourselves. I was once again promised the milk, but hormonally I'm not built to produce it, though three months of fruitless pumping still ensued. But really there's little about my body that says natural fertility. You were made in Beverly Hills in a lab. Not sure how to explain that to you and the photos I have of your embryonic state, but perhaps it avoids the sex question of where do babies come from. Well, you take the sperm and the egg and inject one into the other, wait for them to bind and put them in mummy, but the rest is hocus pocus.

Though my emotions were jumping all over the place, I really wanted nothing more in those five newborn days than just to be together, alone. So we'd take our walks along the hallways I had never had the opportunity to stroll with Reuben. And I stood outside the NICU peering in, reminding myself of the different experience. I wanted those moments to last on and on. If I closed my eyes for a bit, could I stretch the time of their existence?

And now in a heartbeat you are five. You are brave 'til the Grinch jumps out at you. You're funny and sweet when you're vehemently defending your rights and fairness, you're a lover of the company of friends 'til you want some space, naturally curious 'til you're bored, always happy 'til you're mad—the latter you will tell me quite emphatically.

And your accomplishments? Can I say much more than that you are perfectly average? Neither the brightest nor the slowest academically, and just as much the best as the worst sportsman in class. And yet when I push all those aside, what are we left with? One incredibly kind, funny, sensitive, empathetic and giving little boy. I mean knock-my-socks-off sweet—you really are. And you're drawn to sweet friends, not the "rough" ones, but only on the condition that they swear allegiance to Batman and are happy to be playing construction daily.

Your brother is "brother." It feels like a while since he's been "Reuben," you would do anything for him with empathy and understanding until he drives you crazy. When you were born, Reuben at 18 months looked upon you with a measure of quiet and contemplative curiosity. He watched you grow whilst he grew so much slower beside you in stature 'til you reached a plateau together. He, and then, you appeared to grow together at the same rate, clothes being interchangeable between you, the spoken words so similar, intrinsically linked.

You are often described as having an accent, though I'm never quite sure if that means English or American. To me, it's you're voice, with a cute little curl inside it, erupting into a striking gorgeous smile. Oh that smile and those cherry red lips, the cute white and happy teeth, the Irish– blue eyes that reflect the colour of SoCal skies.

Songs. Oh how you want me to make up a new ditty every night, but how it really isn't that tough when I just look at your sleepy contentment. Never one to snuggle a toy to sleep, you love the warmth of family cuddles to send you off to slumber.

You love neighbours and happily talk of them, call out to them, wish to watch them from the windows, peering into their lives, feeling comfort in that snippet of their daily lives being available.

You have your own planet that you have created entirely in your mind. It's called Safay, with the stress on the second "a" and it orbits the Sun as the closest planet to our star. Its red volcanic surface is dotted with trees and construction sites, with the wicked proviso that the trees are always being burnt by the extreme temperature. It has no rings and is the largest of all the planets, being THIS BIG. You can picture it, right?

I wonder what I could think of saying if I had more than the time it takes to be driven home from Disneyland in the passenger seat, those 30 minutes. Perhaps I'll try again tomorrow. For now, did I tell you I love you?

Happy fifth birthday Callum Andreas, my perfectly average son.

Love,
Mummy

I Want You to do The Super-Right Thing

– Peter Katelan

To my dear Victoria,

Over this first year that you are with us, I have from time to time written a few words on this paper. These words are filled with love, and with guidance, with the hopes that they will help you to live a wonderful life. For your mother and me, life is wonderful because you are here.

You can be whatever you want to be.

You will decide what you want, whatever it is. You can change your mind, like your mommy.

You probably will change your mind, like your mommy.

You will be smart enough to know when to change your mind and how to change your situation for the better. As a result of all of this, no one will tell you what to do or what to be.

You will decide for yourself and it will be a great life.

You are going to be smart, but also we want you to always try hard. Always focus on going forward. "What's next?"

The most important thing is to try hard and give your best effort. As grandma always said, "Push yourself."

Remember, someone is always watching – maybe mommy, maybe daddy, grandma, grandpa, someone. So whatever you do, remember, someone is watching you.

You are beautiful on the outside, which we all can see.

You are beautiful on the inside, which is more important. Combining your beauty with your brains is very powerful. You will be very strong, in character and conviction.

Invest in yourself.

Invest in things you control.

Gamble/risk what you don't mind losing tomorrow.

You will have many friends. They will come and go. Very few will stay forever. Have fun with them. But, do not trust them too much. Too many times, they will only want what's good for them, not what's good for you. Always think about what's good for you, because you will be around a long-time – they will not.

But, your parents will always want what's good for you, what's best for you. You may not realize it now. You may not understand it now. You may not like it now, but you will sometime in the future. It's what's best for you so that you may grow up to become a good person.

You will be so many things. You will be a princess; you will be my book buddy; you will be my little warrior; you will be my look out; you will be my assistant. And so many other things also.

Being able to wake up the next day and do exactly what you want is one of the greatest achievements one can have.

If you have something, know that someone else wants it. Protect what you have. Because once it is gone, it is very hard to get it back.

Having good character is very, very important. Good character is doing the right thing when someone is watching and when no one is watching. It is doing the right thing all the time.

Do the right thing, but for you, I want you to do the super– right thing. That is, more than just the right thing. For example, when crossing the street, stop, look a little, and then look a lot.

When speaking with others, use proper English. They will respect you more and treat you better.

Know where you want to go. Remember that destinations may change, but you can only get where you want to go if you know where it is you want to go. And, look where you are going to make sure you are on the right path.

Read and research what you love. Let your passion for what you love take you as far as it can, and this will help you enjoy life.

So my dear daughter, it is with lots of love that I share this with you, because your mother and I wish you a great, joyous life filled with love!!!

Because you have given this to us!!! Happy 1st Birthday

Love,
Peter

Chapter 6

Coming Full Circle

The last two letters in this collection are here at the end of the book because they complete the circle.

When our children are little, we can be like superheroes to them. There's nothing quite like it. Of course we know the truth of the matter, but we're happy to go along with it, for a while at least.

As we grow into our later years, we sense the endless ebb and flow of life. Nothing is constant. Life shapes them, perhaps more strongly than we could ever hope to shape the lives of our children. It is at this time that we need to rekindle our parental super powers.

No matter how old they are, we can help our children grow toward their goals and support them through their failures. This world isn't perfect, but we can be "perfectly imperfect" children and parents. Our children will be fine as long as they know they are loved.

My greatest lessons in life have come from my own mom. I'm grateful for the lessons she taught me and the love she shared, which she is now sharing with all of her grandchildren. The letter written by her is addressed to them.

The final short letter turns things around—it's from the kids this time, written to their parents. To children, love is a simple concept. It doesn't need explanation. They sense it, and they reflect it without any taint of ego or selfishness. It is a true wonder. If you're looking for something extraordinary in life, look no further. It's our duty to nurture and safeguard that most precious thing.

As I read through these letters of those most dear to me, I see that we are so similar, despite our differences. They are special to me because they serve as a reminder of what's most important. Compiling these letters has opened doors in my heart and mind. I hope this book has done the same for you. Here at the last chapter of Love Notes, I invite you to start a new chapter in your life.

We Are All on a Journey in this Huge World We Live In

– Valerie Segil

To my darling grandchildren,

I feel so blessed to have you all in my life. I value your individuality, charm, kindness and character. It means everything to be part of your lives and be able to watch you blossom and grow.

Family is the most important ingredient in life. I hope that you will all love, protect and cherish each other always. There are no ties as strong as family ties. We must never let anything come between us.

A word of caution about money. Money should not make or break a family. If someone needs financial help and you are able to, give them the money as a gift and let it go. If you get repaid down the line, be happy. If you do not get repaid, do not hold a grudge. We have to stand by each other.

My grandpa, Meish, had to flee Russia and settled in Johannesburg, South Africa. He was uneducated but worked very hard near the goldmines. He was well respected by his customers and he was an honest man. He always wanted the best for his children and they were all able to get a good education and made an honest living. When your dads were young I used to take them to visit him and he would give each of your papas a dollar. On our way home we would stop at the BP gas station and your dads would buy a Smurf, which is why you have a collection of Smurfies.

Grandma did not drive so Grandpa Meish used to drive his Pontiac 600 mile for 2 days from Johannesburg to Cape Town to visit us, his family. One day I asked him why he did not fly and he replied that when God wants him he will call for him. He does not need to make it easier by flying so close to heaven. One year he was unable to drive so he flew to Cape Town and enjoyed it so much that he regretted being too old to fly to see the world.

Please make sure to respect your parents. They only want the best for you, even if it doesn't feel that way at the time. Know that they are always looking out only for you.

As Grandma Meish used to say, "Your children are lent to you. After they have grown up they will fly away and then hopefully return to you one day. If this happens consider it a miracle." In reality kids go away to college or explore the world. We hope you will always return to your loving family.

We are fortunate to live in America. All my grandkids are born in America and do not talk funny like Granny Val who says pushchair for stroller, nappies for diapers, lounge for living room and robot for traffic light. Appreciate how fortunate you are to live in the U.S.A. Always care about the people less fortunate than yourself. Have compassion, read to the blind, feed the homeless, donate clothes and toys to the needy, do what you can. Be grateful for what you do have; do not take your good life for granted.

Please do not drink and drive or text and drive or answer the phone when you drive. Remember accidents happen in the blink of an eye and no one is invincible. There are no second chances. STAY SAFE.

Money does not grow on trees. Sometimes you feel it's unfair when you are denied something you want. It is okay NOT to get everything you want or think you need. You will grow to understand this as you become older.

We live in a wonderful country. Both your papas have done very well. All of you grandchildren are loved and treasured. Sometimes life gives us hard knocks and bad things happen. We are a strong, resilient family and will always cope with adversity. If there was never any negative we would not be able to appreciate the positive.

Try to always wake up filled with hope and happiness. Believe in yourself.

Be respectful to all people. Be a good listener.

Be kind.

Remember words can hurt.

Sometimes we do not know the right answer and we need to listen. We are all on a journey in this huge world we live in.

Love,
Granny

You Give Us All A Really Happy Life

– The Segil Family Kids

Dear Mommy and Daddy,

Since it is your 10th anniversary today, Flynn, Natalie and I wanted to write you a special letter to tell you that we love you.

We love mommy because she is nice and caring to everyone. She is also good at baking and cooking. Her shepherd's pie is our favorite because it's made of mashed potatoes and carrots and it's yummy and savory. Thank you mommy for showing up at soccer and baseball games. Also, thank you for always being there for us and getting us new things. Thank you for taking care of Natalie and Flynn. Finally, thank you for always helping me solve problems. This is why I love you mommy.

We love you daddy because you always plan the trips for the family to go to Palm Springs. Thank you for getting all of our baseball and soccer equipment. Also thanks for taking everyone to places, for fun events. You are an amazing father and worker for your business. Thank you for always being there and playing with us.

You have taught us some important lessons in life. 1) To use your words not physical actions to problem solve. 2) We know that we can talk to you about anything. We know you will support us in any situation no matter what. 3) Never give up even though things might seem bad and impossible.

This is why we love you. You give us all a really happy life.

Hugs & kisses,
Jameson, Natalie and Flynn

P.S. Flynn loves you because you get him 1,000 screwdrivers

Send Us Your Letter

This unique project has been an inspiration to so many people that we have decided to turn it into an annual event.

Where you inspired too? We would love to hear from you. If you would like to share your letter, please send us a copy. We will take a look and consider it for inclusion in next year's issue. You don't need to be a professional writer, and it doesn't matter what your background is. The idea is to share the wisdom and love that you have – for the sake of your children.

Parents from around the world have much more in common than we might believe. We want people to think about what is most important, share more positive ideas in the world, write it down, and be a part of it!

You can mail your letter (or any comments and ideas that you feel would be useful and positive) to the following address:

Letters@SegilLoveNotes.com

Dear

Love,

Made in the USA
San Bernardino, CA
28 September 2017